No. ______

In the Supreme Court of the United States

Sam Sloan,
Richard Bozulich,
Thomas R. Stevens,
Petitioners,
-against-

Daniel S. Szalkiewicz,
Salvatore G. Caruso,
Board of Elections in the City of New York,
Attorney General of the State of New York

AF880673

MOTION PURSUANT TO RULE 23.3 FOR STAY OF DECISION TO REMOVE PETITIONER-CANDIDATES FROM THE BALLOT

This proceeding is brought under Election Law Sections 16-100 and 16-102 and other provisions of New York Law. Sam Sloan is a candidate for Mayor of the City of New York. Richard Bozulich is a candidate for Comptroller of the City of New York. Thomas R. Stevens is a candidate for Public Advocate of the City of New York. All are registered Republicans.

Supporters of the candidates circulated petitions and the requisite number of signatures were obtained to get on the ballot. The signed petitions were timely submitted to the Board of Elections in the City of New York. The Petitions complied in every respect with the election rules, including cover sheets and wording of the petitions. There were enough signatures, the cover sheet was done properly and the wording of the petit [illegible] rect.

However, on July 31, 2013, all three of these [illegible] s were thrown off the ballot after a hearing by the New York City [illegible] Elections for one reason only, which was that these were [illegible] for the Republican Party Primary, and the subscribing wi [illegible] tors) were not registered as Republicans with the New York City Bo [illegible] ions.

Unfortunately, the candidates ha [illegible] y aware that there was any rule requiring that the mere wit [illegible] members of any political party. Had they known about this [illegible] e been able to take appropriate action on time (alth [illegible] been difficult as there are few Republicans willing to perfo [illegible] sing signatures which may expose them to civil liability [illegible]

The statute which under the int [illegible] ard of Elections requires the mere witnesses to be Republ [illegible]) of New York Election law states:

> There sha [illegible] bottom of each sheet a signed st [illegible] who is a duly qualified voter of t [illegible] ed voter of the same political [illegible] alified to sign the petition, and who [illegible] e political subdivision in which th [illegible] o be voted for.

This provision was declared unc [illegible] ase Lerman v. Bd. of

Elections of N.Y.C., 2[illegible] F.3d 135, 145 (2d Cir. 2000). This is explained in Dekom vs. New York, 12-CV-[illegible](JS)(AEL).

However, at the hearing of this appeal before the Appellate Division on August 13, 2013 and before a [illegible] of the New York Court of Appeals on April 21, 2013, counsel for the Board of Elections and the Department of Law suggested that the Lerner decision had been overruled by the Maslow case, which is Maslow v. Board of Elections in City of N.Y., 658 F.3d 291 (2d Cir. 2011).

Petitioner-Appellant contends that the Maslow case has nothing to do with the instant case because the Maslow Case was a test case for declaratory relief, not an actual case, whereas in the instant the petitioners have been trying hard to get on the ballot and have spent considerable money to do so, yet have been thwarted by an unwritten rule they had no way to know about.

The First Amendment of the Constitution provides:

> "Congress shall make no law respecting an establishment of religion, or prohibiting the free exercise thereof; or abridging the freedom of speech, or of the press; or the right of the people peaceably to assemble, and to petition the government for a redress of grievances."

Here the law clearly infringes the Constitutional Right "to petition the government". There have been several cases on this subject, but all of them have been federal cases.

The subscribing witness rule was found unconstitutional in Kaloshi v. New York City Board of Elections, 02 CV 4762, 2002 WL 31051530 (E.D.N.Y. Sept. 6, 2002). This is a lengthy and reasoned opinion that declared the specific statute in question to be unconstitutional. This is the only reported case that deals directly with this statute.

It appears from the oral argument held before the Appellate Division that counsel for the Board of Elections would also like to see this case reviewed by this court because he believes the Lerner Decision was effectively overruled by the Maslow decision. The Lerner decision has been a thorn in the side for the Board of Elections as the Board of Elections has difficulty checking voter registrations in Upstate New York and this constantly causes problems in New York City Elections.

The main operative fact is it is undisputed that the petitioners collected 3905 valid signatures whereas only 3750 are required, except that these 3905 signatures were declared invalid because the signatures were not witnessed by Republicans. While there have been several federal cases related to this issue, there has never been a reported state case directly on this issue.

____
Samuel H. Sloan
1664 Davidson Avenue, Apt. 1B
Bronx NY 10453

917-507-7226
917-659-3397
samhsloan@gmail.com

State of New York
Court of Appeals

Decided and Entered on the
twenty-first day of August, 2013

Present, HON. JONATHAN LIPPMAN, *Chief Judge*, ***presiding.***

Mo. No. 2013-900
In the Matter of Sam Sloan,
Appellant,
et al.,
Petitioners,
v.
Daniel S. Szalkiewicz, et al.,
Respondents.

Appellant having moved for leave to appeal to the Court of Appeals in the above cause;

Upon the papers filed and due deliberation, it is

ORDERED, that the motion is denied.

Andrew W. Klein
Clerk of the Court

NEW YO[illegible]ALS

[illegible]
Ri[illegible]
Th[illegible]

[illegible]ppellants,

[illegible]

Danie[illegible],
Sal[illegible]
Board of Electi[illegible] of New York,

[illegible]espondents.

MOTION FOR LEAVE T[illegible] COURT OF APPEALS

Inde[illegible]3

This proceeding is brought u[illegible]Sections 16-100 and 16-102 and other provisions of [illegible] Sloan is a candidate for Mayor of the City of New [illegible]ulich is a candidate for Comptroller of the City [illegible] R. Stevens is a candidate for Public Advocat[illegible]ew York.

Supporters of the candidates [illegible]ons and the requisite number of signat[illegible] were ob[illegible]he ballot. The signed petitions were timely submit[illegible] Elections in the City of New York. The Petitions c[illegible]espect with the election rules, including co[illegible]ding of the petitions.

There were enough signatures, the cover sheet was done properly and the wording of the petition was correct.

However, on July 3[illegible], 2013, all three of these candidates were thrown off the ballot after a hearing by the New York City Board of Elections for one reason only, which was that these were designating petitions for the Republican Party Primary, and the subscribing witnesses (not the subscribers) were not registered as Republicans with the New York City Board of Elections.

Unfortunately, the candidates had not been previously aware that there was any rule requiring that the mere witnesses to a petition be members of any political party. Had they known about this rule they might have been able to take appropriate action on time (although this would have been difficult as there are few Republicans willing to perform this task of witnessing signatures which may expose them to civil liability).

The statute which under the interpretation by the Board of Elections requires the mere witnesses to be Republicans is Section 132 (2) of New York Election law which states:

> There shall be appended at the bottom of each sheet a signed statement of a witness who is a duly qualified voter of the state and an enrolled voter of the same political party as the voters qualified to sign the petition, and who is also a

> resident of the political subdivision in which the office or position is to be voted for.

This provision was declared unconstitutional in the case Lerman v. Bd. of Elections of N.Y.C., 232 F.3d 135, 145 (2d Cir. 2000). This is explained in Dekom vs. New York, 12-CV-1318 (JS)(ARL).

However, at the hearing of this appeal before the Appellate Division on August 13, 2013, counsel for the Board of Elections and the Department of Law suggested that the Lerner decision has been overruled by the Maslow case, which is Maslow v. Board of Elections in City of N.Y., 658 F.3d 291 (2d Cir. 2011).

Petitioner-Appellant contends that the Maslow case has nothing to do with the instant case because the Maslow Case was a test case for declaratory relief, not an actual case, whereas in the instant the petitioners have been trying hard to get on the ballot and have spent considerable money to do so, yet have been thwarted by an unwritten rule they had no way to know about.

The First Amendment to the Constitution provides:

> "Congress shall make no law respecting an establishment of religion, or prohibiting the free exercise thereof; or abridging the freedom of speech, or of the press; or the right of the people peaceably to assemble, and to petition the

government for a redress of grievances."

Here the law clearly infringes the Constitutional Right "to petition the government". There have been several cases on this subject, but all of them have been federal cases. Petitioner maintains that the state courts are just as competent and capable to decide constitutional issues as the federal courts are.

The subscribing witness rule was found unconstitutional in Kaloshi v. New York City Board of Elections, 02 CV 4762, 2002 WL 31051530 (E.D.N.Y. Sept. 6, 2002). This is a lengthy and reasoned opinion that declared the specific statute in question to be unconstitutional. This is the only reported case that deals directly with this statute.

It appears from the oral argument held before the Appellate Division that counsel for the Board of Elections would also like to see this case reviewed by this court because he believes the Lerner Decision was effectively overruled by the Maslow decision. The Lerner decision has been a thorn in the side for the Board of Elections as the Board of Elections has difficulty checking voter registrations in upstate New York and this constantly causes problems in New York City Elections.

The main operative fact is it is undisputed that the petitioners collected 3905 valid signatures [illegible] 750 are required, except that these 3905 signa[illegible]d invalid because the signatures were not witnesse[illegible] While there have been several federal cases relate[illegible] there has never been a reported state case on this [illegible]s motion for leave to appeal should be granted.

NOTE: We have just learned t[illegible]ens is seriously ill and has been hospitalized an[illegible]aring. Richard Bozulich is now out of the country an[illegible] campaign should he get back on the ballot.

____

[illegible]oan

[illegible]n Avenue, Apt. 1B

[illegible]53

[illegible]

[illegible]ail.com

The Followi[illegible]der Was Entered And Filed On August 14, 2013

Richter, J.P., [illegible]net-Daniels, Feinman, Gische, Clark, JJ.

10547 In [illegible] Sloan, Index 101087/13
[illegible]tioner-Appellant,

Rich[illegible]zulich, et al.,
[illegible]tioners,

-against-

Dani[illegible] Szalkiewicz, et al.,
[illegible]pondents-Respondents.

Sam Sloan, appe[illegible] pro se.

Daniel S. Szalk[illegible]cz, New York, respondent pro se, and for Salvatore G. C[illegible], respondent.

Michael A. Car[illegible], Corporation Counsel, New York (Stephen Kitzinger of co[illegible]), for Board of Elections in The City of New York, responde[illegible]

Judgment, [illegible]me Court, New York County (Paul Wooten, J.), entered on or a[illegible] August 9, 2013, unanimously affirmed for the reasons stated [illegible]ooten, J., without costs or disbursements.

No opinion. [illegible]rder filed.

THIS [illegible]TITUTES THE DECISION AND ORDER OF THE SUPREME [illegible]T, APPELLATE DIVISION, FIRST DEPARTMENT.

[illegible]NTERED: AUGUST 14, 2013

CLERK

SUPREME COURT OF THE STATE OF NEW YORK — NEW YORK COUNTY

PRESENT: Paul Wooten, Justice   PART 7

Samuel H. Sloan

-v-

Daniel S. Szalkiewicz

INDEX NO. 101087/13

MOTION DATE

MOTION SEQ. NO. 001

MOTION CAL. NO.

The following papers, numbered 1 to ____ were read on this motion to/for ____

	PAPERS NUMBERED
Notice of Motion/ Order to Show Cause — Affidavits — Exhibits ...	
Answering Affidavits — Exhibits	
Replying Affidavits	

Cross-Motion: ☐ Yes ☐ No

Upon the foregoing papers, it is ordered that this motion is dismissed.

MOTION/CASE IS RESPECTFULLY REFERRED TO JUSTICE FOR THE FOLLOWING REASON(S):

FILED

AUG 09 2013

COUNTY CLERK'S OFFICE
NEW YORK

Dated: 8-9-13

Paul Wooten, J.S.C.

Check one: ☒ FINAL DISPOSITION ☐ NON-FINAL DISPOSITION

Check if appropriate: ☐ DO NOT POST ☐ REFERENCE

August 21, 2013

MOTIONS

2 Mo. No. 2013-908
In the Matter of Garett Armwood, et al.,
Respondents,
v.
John P. McCloy, Jr.,
Appellant,
et al.,
Respondent.

Motion for leave to appeal denied.

2 Mo. No. 2013-907
In the Matter of Lori Cassar, et al.,
Respondents,
v.
Craig A. Larsen,
Appellant,
et al.,
Respondents.

Motion for leave to appeal denied.

2 Mo. No. 2013-899
In the Matter of Ibrahim Fall,
Respondent,
v.
Richard A. Luthmann,
Appellant,
et al.,
Respondent.
(And Another Proceeding.)

Motion for leave to appeal denied.

1 Mo. No. 2013-901
In the Matter of Alan Flacks,
et al.,
Respondents,
v.
Board of Elections in the City of New York,
Appellant.

Leave to appeal denied.

2 Mo. No. 2013-916
In the Matter of Maureen S. Hoerger, et al.,
Appellants,
v.
Thomas J. Spota III,
Respondent,
The Suffolk County Board of Elections,
Respondent.

[illegible] istrict Attorneys Association of the State [illegible] for leave to appear amicus curiae on [illegible] rein granted only to the extent that the [illegible] is accepted as filed.

2 Mo. No. 2013-891
In the Matter of Dagan Lacorte,
Appellant,
v.
Howard L. Cytryn, et al.,
Respondents,
et al.,
Respondent.
(And Another Proceeding.)

Leave to appeal granted.

2 Mo. No. 2013-906
In the Matter of Richard M. Rhoades,
Respondent,
v.
Westchester County Board of Elections,
Respondent,
Evelyn M. McCormack, et al.,
Appellants.
(And Another Proceeding.)

Leave to appeal denied.

1 Mo. No. 2013-[illegible]

In the Matter of Sam Sloan,
Appellant,
et al.,
Petitioners,
v.
Daniel S. Szalkiewicz, et al.,
Respondents.

Motion for leave to appeal denied.

STATE OF NEW YORK
OFFICE OF THE ATTORNEY GENERAL

ERIC T. SCHNEIDERMAN
ATTORNEY GENERAL

BARBARA D. UNDERWOOD
SOLICITOR GENERAL

August 19, 2013

Andrew W. Klein,
Clerk of the Court
Court of Appeals
20 Eagle Street
Albany, NY 12207

RE: *Sloan v. Szalkeiewicz and Bd. of Elections in the City of N.Y.*, N.Y. County Index No. 101087/13

Dear Mr. Klein:

We have received notice pursuant to Executive Law § 71 that petitioner-appellant Samuel H. Sloan seeks in this appeal to challenge the constitutionality of Election Law § 6-132(2).

Please be advised that, after careful consideration, the Office of the Attorney General (OAG) has determined that it will not be participating in the above-entitled matter at this time. Because there are many reasons why the OAG may decide not to participate in a matter, the OAG respectfully suggests that no adverse inference regarding its view of the merits of the constitutional challenge to the State statute, or the nature of the State's interest, be drawn from the OAG's non-participation in this matter at this stage.

The OAG may choose to intervene for purposes of defending the constitutionality of the statute at a later stage. We also would appreciate being advised of any decision in this matter.

Very truly yours,

Steven C. Wu
Deputy Solicitor General
(212) 416-6312

120 BROADWAY, NEW YORK N.Y. 10271-0332 • PHONE (212) 416-8020 • FAX (212) 416-8962 *NOT FOR SERVICE OF PAPERS
http://ag.ny.gov

cc: Samuel H. Sloan
Daniel S. Szalkiewicz, Esq.
Stephen Kitziner, Esq.
Stephen H. Richman, Esq.

OFFICE [illegible]

ERIC T. SCHNEIDERMAN
ATTORNEY GENERAL

BARBARA D. UNDERWOOD
SOLICITOR GENERAL

Honorable Paul Wooten
Supreme Court, New York County
60 Centre Street
New York, NY 10007

RE: *Sloan v. Szalkeiewicz* [illegible] *the City of N.Y.*, Index No. 101057/13

Dear Justice Wooten:

We have received notice [illegible] Law § 71 that petitioner Samuel H. Sloan seeks in this [illegible] the constitutionality of Election Law § 6-132(2).

Please be advised that, afte[illegible] the Office of the Attorney General (OAG) has determined th[illegible]ating in the above-entitled matter at this time. Because ther[illegible] the OAG may decide not to participate in a matter, the OA[illegible] that no adverse inference regarding its view of the merits o[illegible]llenge to the State statute, or the nature of the State's intere[illegible]AG's non-participation in this matter at this stage.

The OAG may choose [illegible]poses of defending the constitutionality of the statute [illegible] note that, pursuant to Executive Law § 71 and CPLR § [illegible] appealed, the OAG must receive another section 71 notice. [illegible]iate being advised of any final decision in this matter.

[illegible]

[illegible]neral

STATE OF NEW YORK
OFFICE OF THE ATTORNEY GENERAL

ERIC T. SCHNEIDERMAN
ATTORNEY GENERAL

BARBARA D. UNDERWOOD
SOLICITOR GENERAL

August 13, 2013

Susan Molina Rojas,
Clerk of the Court
Appellate Division, [illegible] Department
27 Madison Avenue
New York, NY 1001[illegible]

RE: *Sloan [illegible] [illegible]iewicz and Bd. of Elections in the City of N.Y.*, Index No. 101087[illegible]

Dear Ms. Rojas:

We have rece[illegible] notice pursuant to Executive Law § 71 that petitioner-appellant Samuel H[illegible] seeks in this appeal to challenge the constitutionality of Election Law § 6-13[illegible]

Please be adv[illegible] that, after careful consideration, the Office of the Attorney General (OAG) has d[illegible]ined that it will not be participating in the above-entitled matter at this time. [illegible]use there are many reasons why the OAG may decide not to participate in a [illegible] The OAG respectfully suggests that no adverse inference regarding its view [illegible] merits of the constitutional challenge to the State statute, or the nature of the [illegible]'s interest, be drawn from the OAG's non-participation in this matter at this st[illegible]

The OAG m[illegible] choose to intervene for purposes of defending the constitutionality of [illegible] statute at a later stage. We note that, pursuant to Executive Law § 71 a[illegible] CPLR § 1012(b), if this matter is further appealed, the OAG must receive anothe[illegible] [illegible]ion 71 notice. We also would appreciate being advised of any final decision in [illegible] matter.

Very truly yours,

Richard P. Dearing
Deputy Solicitor General
(212) 416-6685

cc: Samuel H. Sloan
Daniel S. Szalkiewicz, Esq.
Stephen Kitziner, Esq.
Stephen H. Richman, Esq.

Samuel H. Sloan
1664 Davidson Ave, Apt. 1B
Bronx NY 10453

Tel. 917-659-3397
917-507-7226
samhsloan@gmail.com

August 15, 2013

Richard P. Dearing
Deputy Solicitor General
120 Broadway
New York NY 10005

Re: Challenge to the Constitutionality of New York Election Law 6-132 (2)
in Sloan vs. Szalkiewicz and Board of Elections in the City of New York

Dear Mr. Richard P. Dearing,

Further with respect to my letter of August 6, 2013, this is to notify you that I am filing a motion to the New York Court of Appeals seaking leave to appeal from the decision yesterday by the Appellate Division, First Department that affirmed without opinion the decision of Judge Wooten of August 9.

The Clerk of the Court of Appeals directed me to inform you that the motion for leave appeal and all other election appeals on that day will be held on August 21 at 8:00 AM in the New York Court of Appeals in Albany NY. If you wish to appear you are to file your brief by noon, August 16, 2013, which is tomorrow.

I am challenging the Constitutionality of a Law of New York State, specifically New York Election Law 6-132 (2).

This law in pertinent part provides:

> There shall be appended at the bottom of each sheet a signed statement of a witness who is a duly qualified voter of the state and an enrolled voter of the same political party as the voters qualified to sign the petition, and who is also a resident of the political subdivision in which the office or position is to be voted for.

This law has already been declared unconstitutional in two cases: Lerman v. Bd. of Elections of N.Y.C., 232 F.3d 135, 145 (2d Cir. 2000) and Kaloshi v. New York City Board of Elections, 02 CV 4762, 2002 WL 31051530 (E.D.N.Y. Sept. 6, 2002)

Very Truly Yours,

Samuel H. Sloan

Copy to:

New York City Board of Elections
32 Broadway
New York NY 10005

[illegible] Apt. 1B
[illegible]

[illegible] 97
[illegible] 26

[illegible] .com

[illegible]

Eric Schneiderman
Attorney General of New York
120 Broadway
New York NY 10005

Re: Challenge to the [illegible] York Election Law 6-132 (2)
in Sloan vs. Szalkiew [illegible] s in the City of New York

Dear Mr. Schneiderman,

This is to notify you that I have filed a cas [illegible] tionality of a Law of New York State, specifically New York Election Law [illegible]

This law in pertinent part provides:

> There shall be appended at [illegible] signed statement of a witness who is a duly qualified voter of t [illegible] oter of the same political party as the voters qualified to sign t [illegible] o a resident of the political subdivision in which the off [illegible] d for.

This law has already been declared uncon [illegible] d. of Elections of N.Y.C., 232 F.3d 135, 145 (2d Cir. 2000). Nevertheless, that [illegible] ded and the Board of Elections in the City of New York continues to enforce [illegible] y.

In my case, I am a registered Republican. [illegible] idates who are also registered Republicans to run for Citywide offices. A [illegible] n signatures were collected and timely filed with the Board of Elections in [illegible] 2 Broadway.

We were taken by surprise when I receive [illegible] from a clerk in the Board of Elections informing me that almost all of [illegible] ered invalid solely because they had not been "witnessed" by an enrolled [illegible] Party. Previously, I thought that any credible person could witness a petiti [illegible] w that there were restrictions and limitations on who could collect or submit [illegible]

My Candidates were kicked off the ballot [illegible] it in New York Supreme Court, New York County, the following day. The [illegible] cz and Board of Elections in the City of New York, Index No. 101087/13.

At a hearing yesterday, August 5, before J [illegible] hattan State Supreme Court I learned that the Board of Elections in the [illegible] g New York Election Law 6-132

(2) as the sole basis for dec[illegible] 3905 of my signatures to be invalid, since the witnesses to those petitions were not registere[illegible]ublicans. I did not personally know any of the petition gatherers except that I met them dur[illegible] the last few days of the petition drive. However, I have since looked them up on the records of t[illegible]ard of Elections and I have found them to be a mixture of Democrats, Libertarians and Blanks. A[illegible]em are registered voters. Mostly they seem to be people who have little interest in politics but [illegible] gather petition signatures as a means of employment.

As the hearing in Manhatta[illegible]preme Court yesterday, counsel for the Board of Elections stated that this provision of New York [illegible] has been found to be Constitutional in three federal cases. However, I have been able to locate an[illegible] up two of these three cases and have found that they do not apply to my case.

The main case cited by Cou[illegible] for the Board of Elections is Maslow v. Board of Elections in City of N.Y. , 658 F.3d 291 (2d Cir. [illegible] citing N.Y. State Bd. of Elections v. Lopez-Torres, 552 U.S. 196, 128 S.Ct. 791, 798, 169 L.Ed.2d [illegible] 2008)

However, the Maslow case [illegible]pletely different from the case presented here. The Maslow case involved Democrats who w[illegible] to register Republicans to run as Republican candidates. For example a bunch of Democrats coul[illegible]ct and submit petitions on behalf of a candidate who is likely to be disruptive to the opponent'[illegible]ans. Naturally, the Republicans would want these people kept out.

However, in my case the pe[illegible]rs were a random collection of semi-homeless Democrats, Libertarians and Blanks w[illegible]re unemployed and simply wanted a job. They had no idea about raiding an opposing party. [illegible] Maslow case, Lori Maslow, the good wife, wanted to be able to circulate petitions on behal[illegible]r husband, Aaron Maslow should he ever decide to run for election as a Republican, even though [illegible] a Democrat. She claimed the Constitutional Right to Associate with the Republican Party even [illegible]h she was not a member of that Party. Her application failed for obvious reasons.

In fact, Aaron Maslow has [illegible] run for office as a Republican and Lori Maslow has never circulated petitions for him as a Dem[illegible] so there was no actual case or controversy.

In the case presented here, [illegible]r, 3905 Republicans signed petitions believing that they were nominating candidates to r[illegible] office as Republicans. The 3905 people who signed the petitions presumably did not know t[illegible]nesses or even who the witnesses would be. They all just naturally assumed that their petition[illegible]valid.

So, it is the constitutional r[illegible] the petitioners that have been infringed. In the Maslow case there were no petitioners because [illegible] petitions had actually been circulated. The Maslow case was merely an action for declar[illegible] relief. It did not occur in the context of an actual controversy. The Maslow case lasted 5 years. [illegible] filed in 2006 and continued until 2011.

The First Amendment to th[illegible]nstitution provides:

> **Congress sha[illegible] no law respecting an establishment of religion, or prohibiting the free exercise [illegible] or abridging the freedom of speech, or of the press; or the right of the people pe[illegible]y to assemble, and to petition the government for a redress of grievances.**

Here the law clearly infring[illegible] Constitutional Right “to petition the government”. No plaintiff in the Maslow case asserted th[illegible]ht because no petition was actually circulated and thus there were no petitioners.

The provision relied upon by the Board of Elections has already been declared unconstitutional in the case Lerman v. Bd. of Elections of N.Y.C., 232 F.3d 135, 145 (2d Cir. 2000).

That decision struck down the sentence cited by the Board of Elections, yet they shamelessly quoted and read from that invalid statute during the hearing on August 5. Although that decision refers to the residency requirement, the residency requirement is in the same sentence as the requirement that a witness must be a member of the same political party and the same logic and reasoning applies. Nevertheless, the statute has not been amended or changed and they read the sentence in full in the hearing before Judge Wooten yesterday.

The Maslow case was pending before the courts for five years, because there was no live controversy and there was no rush to decide it. In the case here however, the Primary Election will be held on September 10. Either the candidates will be on it, or they will not be on it, so a final decision must be made by that time.

It was not until the hearing yesterday that it became apparent that the constitutionality of the Election Law would be the main issue of the case. I raised or attempted to raise other issues, including the apparent forgery of the signature of Salvatore Caruso on the Specific Objections. I also objected to the appearance of Daniel Szalkiewicz as counsel for Salvatore Caruso when it is obvious that Sal Caruso, who is an elderly man approaching 70, is not the real objector and is merely a front man for the undisclosed real objector.

However, these objections were brushed aside and dismissed by Judge Paul Wooten. Nevertheless, I ask you to investigate these matters, including especially the forgery, as the relevant signatures are included in my affidavit, a copy of which I have served on your office.

It is obvious that New York Election Law 6-132 (2) is unconstitutional as applied in this case. Here, we have 3905 voters who signed a petition thinking that it would be submitted to the Board of Elections and the names of the candidates nominated would be on the ballot. The signers did not know anything about the subscribing witnesses and had no connection with them. They did not even know their names much less their political affiliations. It is clear that the 3905 signers of the petitions have the First Amendment constitutional right to petition and these rights have been infringed on the pretext that the witnesses with whom they have no connection are not Republicans. Frankly, this situation is so unconstitutional that I believe that you will not be able to defend it.

Very Truly Yours,

Samuel H. Sloan
(Your next Mayor Provided
I can get back on the Ballot)

Copy to:

New York City Board of Elections
32 Broadway
New York NY 10005

At a Special Election Part
of The Supreme Court of the State
of New York, New York County,
Borough of Manhattan, City of New
York, on the 1st
day of August, 2013

Present: DEBORAH A. KAPLAN, J.S.C.

Samuel H. Sloan,
Richard Bozulich,
Thomas R. Stevens,

Petitioners,

-against-

Daniel S. Szalkiewicz,
Salvatore G. Caruso,
Board of Elections in the City of New York,

Respondents.

101087/13

ORDER TO SHOW CAUSE

Upon the annexed petition of Samuel H. Sloan duly verified the 1st day of August, 2013 and upon all of the papers and proceedings had herein it is hereby

ORDERED that the Respondents show cause before this court at a Special Election Part ~~in~~ 7 Room 341 thereof to be held at the County Courthouse in the Borough of Manhattan at 60 Centre Street, New York NY on the 5th Day of August, 2013 at 9:30AM of that day or as soon thereafter as counsel can be heard why an order should not be made and entered herein

Restoring Sam Sloan to the [illegible] ...ican Candidate for

Mayor of the City of New York a[illegible]

Restoring Richard Bozulich [illegible] a Republican

Candidate for Comptroller of th[illegible] and

Restoring Thomas R. Steven[illegible] a Republican

Candidate for Public Advocate [illegible] York

AND why petitioners should [illegible] ...er and further

relief as may seem just and pro[illegible]s;

Sufficient Cause appearing [illegible] ...further

ORDERED that service of a [illegible] to show cause

together with a copy of the pa[illegible] is based be served

by personal delivery to the Board of El[illegible] of New York at 32

Broadway, New York NY on ~~or be~~ [illegible] by 5:00 [illegible] ...ust 1st, 2013 before 5pm and

upon the other respondents by personal [illegible] ...ices of Daniel S.

Szalkiewicz attorney for the r[illegible] Midnight on August 1st,

2013 or otherwise by personal ~~certified~~ [illegible] ...dual Respondents by 12:00 Midnight on August 2013, ...d and sufficient

service.

[illegible]

[signature]

[illegible] C.

...NAH A. KAPLAN

J.S.C.

SUPREME COURT OF THE STATE OF NEW YORK
COUNTY OF NEW YORK

Sam Sloan,
Richard Bozulich,
Thomas R. Stevens,

Petitioners,

-against-

101087/13

Daniel S. Szalkiewicz,
Salvatore G. Calise,
Board of Elections in the City of New York,

Respondents.

VALIDATING PETITION in New York Election Law

STATE OF NEW YORK :
: SS
COUNTY OF NEW YORK :

Samuel H. Sloan being duly sworn, deposes and says

1. This proceeding is brought under Election Law Sections 16-100 and 16-102 and other provisions of New York Law. No prior application has been made for the relief requested herein.

2. As more fully set forth in the accompanying affidavit, I am a candidate for Mayor of the City of New York. Richard Bozulich is a candidate for Comptroller of the City of New York. Thomas R. Stevens is a candidate for Public Advocate of the City of New York. We are all registered Republicans and thus seek to be on the ballot as Republican party candidates although none of us are members of any

insider clique or group within the Republican Party. We are outsiders as far as the Republican Party is concerned.

3. Designating petitions were circulated in accordance with New York Election Law nominating us as candidates for the above mentioned offices. These petitions were filed with the Board of Elections in the City of New York at 11:50 PM on July 11, 2013. Under the new rules, it is required that petitions with 3750 or more valid signatures be filed. More than enough of the required number of signatures were filed.

4. On July 15, 2013 at 5:35 PM an objector named Sal Caruso filed a "General Objection" with the New York City Board of Elections. These objections were filed one day late as New York Election Law requires that they be filed within three days (not within three business days) of the filing of the petitions. A copy of this General Objection is annexed hereto and Marked Exhibit A.

5. On July 22, 2013, Sal Caruso filed "Specific Objections" with the Board of Elections in the City of New York. These objections were filed one day late as New York Election Law requires that they be filed within six days after the General Objections were filed (not within six business days). A copy of the cover sheet of these Specific Objections is annexed hereto and Marked Exhibit B.

6. The Sal Caruso who filed these General Objections and Specific Objections was and is represented by attorney Daniel S. Szalkiewicz, PC, 280 Riverside Drive, New York, NY 10025.

7. These Objections were facially and obviously invalid for numerous reasons and thus should not have been considered by the Board of Elections in the City of New York.

8. Rather than provide line-by-line specific objections, the objectors claimed that there were 4269 signatures but only 69 were good and the other 4200 were false. They simply marked virtually all of the approximately 500 pages of petition sheets with SWNR, SWNE and marked virtually all of the lines with NR, NE. SWNR means Subscribing Witness not Registered. SWNE means Subscribing Witness not Enrolled.

9. It was quickly established that this was not true. All of the Subscribing witnesses are and were registered to vote in the State of New York. Once this was established, it should have been evident that the Specific Objections were spurious and frivolous and the objectors had never bothered to look up the actual signature cards on file with the Board of Elections. The objectors simply sought to require the Board of Elections and the candidates to do all the work to prove the validity of the petitions. This shifting of the Burden of Proof was improper and should not have been allowed.

10. Nevertheless, the Board of Electi [illegible] ahead with validating the petitions, expending considerable [illegible] effort and resources to do so. The end result was [illegible] the signers were found to be not registered to vote [illegible] more than 4000 signers were found to be not [illegible]ublicans. These numbers were completely different fr[illegible]med by the objectors.

11. However, the Board of El[illegible] in the cases of 3905 of the signatures, although [illegible]egistered Republicans, the subscribing witnesses we[illegible]Republicans.

12. It is an interpretation [illegible]on although not specifically stated in the l[illegible] to the petition must also be in the same politica[illegible]ners. The petitioners here were not aware of this [illegible] the time of circulating these petitions. Petitioners [illegible] this is not strictly speaking what the law says a[illegible]Constitutionally invalid in that it deprives [illegible] candidates of the Constitutional Right to Free[illegible] and has no rational basis. It deprives the signe[illegible]ers the right to nominate candidates of their [illegible]

13. The Specific Objections [illegible]use they contain a forgery. What purports to be [illegible]Salvatore Caruso at the bottom of the Specific Objec[illegible]nd obviously not the

signature of the person who signed the General Objection, nor it is the signature of the person who signed the Voter Registration Card of Sal Caruso. Other than the initial letter S there is no similarity between the signatures.

14. There can be little doubt that the person who forged the signature of Sal Caruso is the attorney who filed the objections, Daniel S. Szalkiewicz, PC, 280 Riverside Drive, New York, NY 10025.

15. Accordingly, petitioner suggests that this matter be referred to the DA regarding the forgery. Respondents Daniel S. Szalkiewicz and Salvatore G. Caruso should be required to appear and submit their signatures for handwriting analysis and be required to testify as to whom signed these general and specific objections.

16. An article in the New York Daily News dated July 22, 2013 stated that 20 pages of signature petitions for Republican Party Candidate for Comptroller Joe Burnett were "accidentally" shredded by workers at the Board of Elections but that the candidate was allowed to reconstruct these 20 pages so that his name will appear on the ballot. According to this article, this shredding pf the signatures was related to a turf war between GOP insiders Chairman Craig Eaton and State Senator Martin Golden and that the appointment of Board of Elections Commissioner Simon Shamoun was the result of a "power grab" by a faction of the Republican Party. This same person was among

those who voted at a Board of Elections hearing on July 29, 2013 not to allow the names of above petitioners Sloan, Bozulich and Stevens to appear on the Citywide ballot. In view of these obvious irregularities and the obvious conflicts iof interest. This court should order that the names of Sloan, Bozulich and Stevens to appear on the ballot to allow the Republican general electorate decide these issues especially since Sloan, Bozulich and Stevens are complete outsiders and not part of any Republican insider clique or group. A copy of the Daily News Article is annexed hereto as an exhibit.

17. Section 132 (2) of New York Election law provides the following:

> **2. There shall be appended at the bottom of each sheet a signed** statement of a witness who is a duly qualified voter of the state and an enrolled voter of the same political party as the voters qualified to sign the petition, and who is also a resident of the political subdivision in which the office or position is to be voted for. However, in the case of a petition for election to the party position of member of the county committee, residence in the same county shall be sufficient. Such a statement shall be accepted for all purposes as the equivalent of an affidavit, and if it contains a material false statement, shall subject the person signing it to the same penalties as if he or she had been duly sworn. The form of such statement shall be substantially as follows:
>
> STATEMENT OF WITNESS
>
> I,.................... (name of witness) state: I am a duly qualified voter of the State of New York and am an enrolled voter of the...................... party. I now reside at..................
> (residence address).

18. It is apparently the interpretation of the Board of Elections in the City of New York that the above provision implies that the party of the subscribing witness must be the same as the party of the

signer of the petition. However, the above provision does not actually say that. It merely suggests but does not require that the subscribing witness disclose the name of any political party he belongs to, which may be Democrat, Republican, Socialist, Communist, Blank or any other. Nowhere in this provision or anywhere else in New York Law is there a requirement that the mere witness to the signing of a petition be a member of any particular political party. If there were such a provision it would be constitutionally invalid as depriving the right of Freedom of Association and depriving the general membership of the right to chose the candidates they want to run for election.

19. Petitioners are new candidates who have never appeared on the ballot before in any election. We have never circulated Designating Petitions for any party or election previously. Politics in general in New York City and politics in the Republican Party in particular are long dominated by machine politics and by insiders who do not allow outsiders in unless they buy their way in as for example did the current mayor and one of the leading Republican Party candidates. At the same time the Republican Party has been demolished in every recent election and cannot get anybody elected. Nevertheless, they jealously guard the right to control who gets their nomination to insure that only their insider losers get on the ballot. This should not be allowed and the courts should start the opening up of the election process by allowing these three candidates on the ballot.

WHEREFORE, for all of the re[illegible]ve, Petitioner prays

(a) That an order be entered [illegible]oan, Richard Bozulich and Thomas R. S[illegible] as can[illegible]ot in the coming elections

(b) That this matter be refe[illegible]t Attorney's office to investigate the apparent and [illegible] the signature of Salvatore G. Ca[illegible] on the S[illegible]

[illegible]an

Sworn to Before me this 1st
Day of August 2013

____
NOTARY PUBLIC

[illegible]an
[illegible] Avenue, Apt. 1B
[illegible]3

[illegible]l.com

STATE OF NEW YORK)
) ss
COUNTY OF NEW YORK)

I, the undersigned, the peti[illegible] foregoing petition, being duly sworn, says:

I have read the foregoing pe[illegible] me and know the contents thereof and the sam[illegible] knowledge, except as to those matters herein stat[illegible]on information and belief and as to those matte[illegible]be true.

[illegible]re of Petitioner

On the 1st Day of August, 20[illegible]ally came Samuel H. Sloan to me known to be the [illegible]rein and who executed the foregoing instrument. Su[illegible] to such instrument before me and duly acknowled[illegible] the same.

____
NOTARY PUBLIC

[illegible]w York
[illegible]19
[illegible]ounty
[illegible]7, 2014

SUPREME COURT [illegible] THE STATE OF NEW YORK
COUNTY OF NEW [illegible]

Sam Sloan,
Richard Bozuli[illegible]
Thomas R. Stev[illegible]

Petitioners,

01087-2013

-against-

Daniel S. Szal[illegible]z,
Salvatore G. C[illegible],
Board of Elect[illegible] in the City of New York,

Respondents.

AFFIDAVIT IN S[illegible] OF ORDER TO SHOW CAUSE

STATE OF NEW YO[illegible] :
: SS
COUNTY OF NEW Y[illegible] :

Samuel H. Sloan [illegible]ing duly sworn, deposes and says

1. This proceed[illegible] is brought under Election Law Sections 16-100 and 16-102 and othe[illegible]visions of New York Law. No prior application has been made for t[illegible] relief requested herein.

2. I am a candi[illegible] for Mayor of the City of New York. Richard Bozulich is a c[illegible]date for Comptroller of the City of New York. Thomas R. Steve[illegible] a candidate for Public Advocate of the City of New York. We ar[illegible] registered Republicans and thus seek to be on the ballot as R[illegible]lican party candidates although none of us are members of any [illegible]er clique or group within the Republican Party.

We are outsiders as far as the Republican Party is concerned.

3. Designating petitions were circulated in accordance with New York Election Law nominating us as candidates for the above mentioned offices. These petitions were timely filed with the Board of Elections in the City of New York at 11:50 PM on July 11, 2013. Under the new rules, it is required that petitions with 3750 or more valid signatures be filed. More than enough of the required number of signatures were filed.

4. On July 15, 2013 at 5:35 PM an objector named Sal Caruso filed a "General Objection" with the New York City Board of Elections. These objections were filed one day late as New York Election Law requires that they be filed within three days (not within three business days) of the filing of the petitions. A copy of this General Objection is annexed hereto and Marked Exhibit A.

5. On July 22, 2013, Sal Caruso filed "Specific Objections" with the Board of Elections in the City of New York. These objections were filed one day late as New York Election Law requires that they be filed within six days after the General Objections were filed (not within six business days). A copy of the cover sheet of these Specific Objections is annexed hereto and Marked Exhibit B.

6. The Sal Caruso who filed these General Objections and Specific

Objections was and is represented by attorney Daniel S. Szalkiewicz, PC, 280 Riverside Drive, New York, NY 10025.

7. These Objections were facially and obviously invalid for numerous reasons and thus should not have been considered by the Board of Elections in the City of New York.

8. Rather than provide line-by-line specific objections, the objectors claimed that there were 4269 signatures but only 69 were good and the other 4200 were false. The objectors simply marked virtually all of the approximately 500 pages of petition sheets with SWNR, SWNE and marked virtually all of the lines with NR, NE. SWNR means Subscribing Witness not Registered. SWNE means Subscribing Witness not Enrolled.

9. It was quickly established that this was not true. All of the Subscribing witnesses are and were registered to vote in the State of New York. Once this was established, it should have been evident that the Specific Objections were spurious and frivolous and the objectors had never bothered to look up the actual signature cards on file with the Board of Elections. The objectors simply sought to require the Board of Elections and the candidates to do all the work to prove the validity of the petitions. This shifting of the Burden of Proof was improper and should not have been allowed.

10. Nevertheless, the Board [illegible] ahead with validating the petitions, expending con[illegible] effort and resources to do so. The end result was [illegible] the signers were found to be not registered to vote [illegible] more than 4000 signers were found to be not [illegible]ublicans. These numbers were completely different fr[illegible]med by the objectors.

11. However, the Board of El[illegible] in the cases of 3905 of the signatures, although [illegible]egistered Republicans, the subscribing witnesses we[illegible] Republicans.

12. It is an interpretation [illegible]on although not specifically stated in the l[illegible] to the petition must also be in the same politica[illegible]ners. The petitioners herein were not aware of thi[illegible] the time of circulating these petitions. [illegible] believe that this is not strictly speaking what t[illegible] any case is Constitutionally invalid in [illegible]he signers and the candidates of the Constituti[illegible]dom of Association and has no rational basis. It de[illegible] of the petitioners of the right to nominate candid[illegible]choosing.

13. The Specific Objections [illegible]use they contain a forgery. What purports to be [illegible] Salvatore Caruso at the bottom of the Specific Objec[illegible]nd obviously not the

signature of the same person who signed the General Objection, nor it is the signature of the person who signed the Voter Registration Card of Salvatore Caruso. Other than the initial letter S there is no similarity between the signatures.

14. There can be little doubt that the person who forged the signature of Sal Caruso is the attorney who filed the objections, Daniel S. Szalkiewicz, PC, 280 Riverside Drive, New York, NY 10025.

15. Accordingly, petitioner suggests that this matter be referred to the DA regarding this forgery. Respondents Daniel S. Szalkiewicz and Salvatore G. Caruso should be required to appear and submit their signatures for handwriting analysis and be required to testify as to whom signed these general and specific objections.

16. An article in the New York Daily News dated July 22, 2013 stated that 20 pages of signature petitions for Republican Party Candidate for Comptroller John Burnett were "accidentally" shredded by workers at the Board of Elections but that the candidate was allowed to reconstruct these 20 pages so that his name will appear on the ballot. According to this article, this shredding pf the signatures was related to a turf war between GOP insiders Chairman Craig Eaton and State Senator Martin Golden and that the appointment of Board of Elections Commissioner Simon Shamoun was the result of a "power grab" by a faction of the Republican Party. This same person was among

those who voted at a Board of Elections hearing on July 29, 2013 not to allow the names of above petitioners Sloan, Bozulich and Stevens to appear on the Citywide ballot. In view of these obvious irregularities and the obvious conflicts of interest, this court should order that the names of Sloan, Bozulich and Stevens to appear on the ballot to allow the Republican general electorate decide these issues, especially since Sloan, Bozulich and Stevens are complete outsiders and not part of any Republican insider clique or group. A copy of the Daily News Article is annexed hereto as an exhibit.

17. Section 132 (2) of New York Election law provides the following:

> **2. There shall be appended at the bottom of each sheet a signed** statement of a witness who is a duly qualified voter of the state and an enrolled voter of the same political party as the voters qualified to sign the petition, and who is also a resident of the political subdivision in which the office or position is to be voted for. However, in the case of a petition for election to the party position of member of the county committee, residence in the same county shall be sufficient. Such a statement shall be accepted for all purposes as the equivalent of an affidavit, and if it contains a material false statement, shall subject the person signing it to the same penalties as if he or she had been duly sworn. The form of such statement shall be substantially as follows:
>
> STATEMENT OF WITNESS
>
> I,..................... (name of witness) state: I am a duly qualified voter of the State of New York and am an enrolled voter of the...................... party. I now reside at...................
> (residence address).

18. It is apparently the interpretation of the Board of Elections in the City of New York that the above provision implies that the party of the subscribing witness must be the same as the party of the

signer of the petition. However, the above provision does not actually say that. It merely suggests but does not require that the subscribing witness disclose the name of any political party he belongs to, which may be Democrat, Republican, Socialist, Communist, Blank or any other. Nowhere in this provision or anywhere else in New York Law is there a requirement that a mere witness to the signing of a petition be a member of any particular political party. If there were such a provision, it would be constitutionally invalid as depriving the right of Freedom of Association and depriving the general membership of the right to chose the candidates they want to run for election.

19. Petitioners are new candidates who have never appeared on the ballot before in any election. We have never circulated Designating Petitions for any party or election previously. Politics in general in New York City and politics in the Republican Party in particular are long dominated by machine politics and by insiders who do not allow outsiders in unless they buy their way in as for example did the current mayor and one of the leading Republican Party candidates. At the same time, the Republican Party has been demolished in every recent election and cannot get anybody elected. Nevertheless, they jealously guard the right to control who gets their nomination to insure that only their insider losers get on the ballot. This should not be allowed and the courts should start the opening up of the election process by allowing the three petitioners on the ballot.

WHEREFORE, for all of th[illegible] above, Petitioner prays

(a) That an order be ent[illegible]m Sloan, Richard Bozulich and Thomas R. Stevens as [illegible] ballot in the coming elections

(b) That this matter be [illegible]strict Attorney's office to investigate the apparent [illegible]y of the signature of Salvatore G. Caruso on t[illegible]ons.

[illegible] Sloan

Sworn to Before me this [illegible]
Day of August 2013

NOTARY PUBLIC
[illegible] DONG
Notary Public State of New York
Reg. No. [illegible]D06228919
Qualified in New York County
Commission Expires Sept. 27, 2014

[illegible] Sloan
[illegible]dson Avenue, Apt. 1B
[illegible] 10453

[illegible]226
[illegible]397
[illegible]gmail.com

STATE OF NEW YORK

ss:

COUNTY OF NEW YORK

[illegible]TION

I, the undersigned, the [illegible] the foregoing petition, being duly sworn, says:

I have read the foregoing [illegible]ed by me and know the contents thereof and the [illegible] own knowledge, except as to those matters herein [illegible]d upon information and belief and as to those m[illegible] to be true.

[illegible]nature of Petitioner

On the 1st Day of August [illegible] personally came Samuel H. Sloan to me known to be [illegible]d herein and who executed the foregoing instrument [illegible] swore to such instrument before me and duly ackno[illegible]cuted the same.

NOTARY PUBLIC

[illegible] DONG
[illegible]e of New York
[illegible]06228919
[illegible] York County
[illegible] Sept. 27, 2014

Exhibit A

General Objection of Sal Caruso to the Candidacy of Sam S[illegible] for Mayor of New York City

BX 34

GENERAL OBJECTION

TO: The Board of Elections in the City of New York

OBJECTOR: Name: Sal Caruso

Residence Address: 540 Ellsworth Ave

Bronx, New York 10465

OBJECTOR'S CONTACT PERSON:

Note: The Objector may name himself or herself as the contact person

Name: Law Offices of Daniel S Szalkiewicz, P.C.

Mailing Address: 280 Riverside Dr.

(may be a business address) New York NY 10025

Telephone Numbers: 212 706 1007

Fax Number: 914 500 2315

2013 JUL 15 PM 5:35

G.O. BD. OF ELECTION IN THE CITY OF NEW YORK 32 BROADWAY

The objector hereby objects to the designating/independent nominating petition which was filed with the Board of Elections which purports to name the following as a candidate in the Primary/General/Special Election to be held on September 10, 2013 for the office indicated:

CANDIDATE: Name: Sam Sloan

Residence Address: 1664 Davidson Ave

Bronx NY 10453

Public Office or Party Position: Mayor of the City of New York

District: City wide

Political Party: Republican

Salvatore Caruso

Objector's Signature

Exhibit B

Specific Objection of Sal Caruso to the Candidacy of Sam Sloan for Mayor of New York City

Note that the signature on the General Objection of Sal Caruso is completely different from the signature of Sal Caruso on the Specific Objection

SPECIF[illegible] [illegible]NT

TO: The Board of Elections in the [illegible]

OBJECTOR: Name: [illegible]

Residence Address: [illegible]

OBJECTOR'S CONTACT PERSON

Name: [illegible]zalkiewicz

Mailing Address: [illegible]erside Drive
(only use business address)

[illegible] NY 10025

Telephone Number: [illegible] 1007

Fax Number: [illegible] 2315

Indicate if there is a different fax number to be used [illegible]

The objector submits the following [illegible] of the General Objection to the nominating petition for:

CANDIDATE: Name: [illegible]

Residence Address: [illegible]dson Ave

[illegible] York 10453

Public Office or Pa[illegible] [illegible] of the City of New

District: [illegible]E

Political Party/Inde[illegible] [illegible]blican Party

PETITION VOLUME IDENTIFICAT[illegible]

[illegible] NY 30234

[illegible] NY 30238

[illegible]

(CANDIDATE'S CONTACT PERSO[illegible] sheet):

Name: [illegible]

Mailing Address: [illegible] Ave, Bronx NY [illegible]

Telephone Number: [illegible]

Fax Number: [illegible]

TOTAL NUMBER OF SIGNATURE[illegible] 4269

NUMBER OF INVALID SIGNATUR[illegible] 4200

The line by line and any other spec[illegible] d.

[signature]

Objector's Signature

Exhibit C

Voter Registration Card of Salvatore Caruso

Note that the signature on the Voter Registration Card of Salvatore Caruso is similar to the signature of Sal Caruso on the General Objection but is completely different from the signature of Sal Caruso on the Specific Objections

Board of Elections in the City of New York

☐ Yes, I need an application for an Absentee Ballot **Please print or type in blue or black ink** ☐ Yes, I would like to be an Election Day Worker

1 Are you a U.S. citizen? Yes ☑ No ☐
If you answered NO, do not complete this form.

2 I will be 18 years old on or before election day: Yes ☑ No ☐
If you answered NO, do not complete this form, unless you will be 18 by the end of the year.

For Board use only!
BOARD OF ELECTIONS NEW YORK CITY G.O.
HAVA
2004 OCT

3 Last Name: CARUSO | First Name: SALVATORE | Middle Initial: | Suffix:

4 Address Where You Live (do not give P.O. address): 540 Ellsworth Ave | Apt. No.: C1 | City/Town/Village: Bronx. N.Y. | Zip Code: 10465 | County: Bronx

5 Address Where You Get Your Mail (if different from above) | P.O. box, star rte., etc. | Post Office | Zip Code

6 Date of Birth: 9-9-46

7 Sex (circle): (M) F

8 Home Tel. Number (optional)

9 ID Number - Check the applicable box and provide your number
☑ New York Driver's License Number ☐ Last four digits of your Social Security number
→ 353 155 664
☐ I do not have a New York driver's license number or a Social Security number.

10 The last year you voted: 12 YRS
Your Address was (give house number, street, and city): 3170 Layton Ave Bronx. NY 10465
In county/state: Bronx N.Y.
Under the name (if different from your name now)

11 Choose a Party — Check one box only
☑ REPUBLICAN PARTY
☐ DEMOCRATIC PARTY
☐ INDEPENDENCE PARTY
☐ CONSERVATIVE PARTY
☐ WORKING FAMILIES PARTY
☐ OTHER (write in)________
☐ I DO NOT WISH TO ENROLL IN A PARTY

Please note: In order to vote in a **primary election,** you must be enrolled in one of these parties.

12 **AFFIDAVIT:** I swear or affirm that
- I am a citizen of the United States.
- I will have lived in the county, city, or village for at least 30 days before the election.
- I meet all requirements to register to vote in New York State.
- This is my signature or mark on the line below.
- The above information is true. I understand that if it is not true I can be convicted and fined up to $5,000 and/or jailed for up to four years.

⬇ Signature or mark ⬇

x Salvatore Caruso Date OCT. 4-04

Please do not write in this space

Eng 12/03

Exhibit D

Cover sheet as Amended of Designating Petitions filed by Sam Sloan

S... AMI ... SHEET

Designating and Independent Petitions ... Counties which Utilize Petition Identification Numbering Systems

K... PARTY

~~[Place Name of~~ ... ~~Body Here]~~

Name of Candidate	Public Office or Party ...	...ss (also mailing address if different)
SAM SLOAN	MAYOR OF ...	... DAVIDSON AVE BRONX NY ...
RICHARD GORDON	COMPTROLLER	... END AVE NEW YORK NY 1...
THOMAS R. STEVENS	PUBLIC ...	... 194TH ST FLUSHING NY 11...

Total Number of Volumes in Petition ...

Identification Numbers NY1301283, ... 284, NY1301285, NY130128... NY1301287, NY1301288, ... 01290, NY1301291

The petition contains the number, or in ... valid signatures required by the Election Law.

Contact Person to Correct Deficiencies

Name: SAM SLOAN
(please print)

Residence Address: 1664 DAVID...
BRONX NY ...

... erent)

Phone: ...659-33...

I hereby authorize that notice of any de... Board of Elections be transmitted to the person named above:

SAM SLOAN

Candidate or Agent

"This is to certify that I am authorized t... sheet."

JULY 17, 2013

Date

[signature] Signature

INSTRUCTIONS: *Clearly identify the or... mended or attach a copy of the original cover sh...*

2013 JUL 17 PM 2:04
... IN THE CITY OF NEW YORK
32 BROADWAY

Exhibit E

Clerk's Report in the Matter of the Objections by Sal Caruso

This clerk's report shows that 3903 of the signatures were found to be valid, more than the required number, except that the interpretation of the Board of Elections is that the signers are "Not Enrolled in Party (NE) (SW-NE)"

CLERK'S REPORT

Party Republican

BRONX County Date: 7/25/2013

Petition Identification Numbers	
	NY1301282; NY1301283; NY1301284; NY1301285
	NY1301286; NY130287; NY1301288
	NY13011289; NY1301290; NY1301291

Spec. No.

In the Matter of the Objections by Sal Caruso (Objector) to the Petition of Sam Sloan (Candidate) for Mayor - Citywide

PART I. REASONS FOR INVALIDATION OF SIGNATURES

	Signature Area	Witness Statement
Address Illegible (AI) (SW-AI)	9	0
Alteration of Date/Signature (ALT) (SW-ALT)	10	0
Date Incomplete (DI) (SW-DI)	0	0
Duplicate-Same Petition (DUP)	0	
Date of Witness Statement Prior to Signature (DSP)	0	
Illegible Signature (ILLS) (SW-ILLS)	0	0
Illegible Date (ILLD) (SW-ILLD)	0	0
No Address Stated (NA) (SW-NA)	3	0
No Date Stated (ND) (SW-ND)	0	0
Not Enrolled in Party (NE) (SW-NE)	59	3905
No First Name (NFN) (SW-NFN)	0	0
No Page Number (NPN)	0	
Not Registered (NR) (SW-NR)	112	110
Out of the District of Contest (OD) (SW-OD)	0	0
Pencil or Not in Ink (P) (SW-P)	0	0
Printed Not Handwritten (PR) (SW-PR)	0	0
Signed Another Petition for Same Office (SAP)	0	
Subscribing Witness Also Signator (SW)	0	
Subscibing Witness Name Omitted (SW-NN)		0
Subscribing Witnesss Wrong # of Signatures (SWWNS)		0
Subscribing Witness Signature Missing (SW-NS)		0
Date of Signature Prior to First Day to Circulate (TE) (SW-TE)	0	0
Date of Signature After Last Day to Circulate (TL) (SW-TL)	0	0
Other:		
Totals	193	4015
Total Invalid Signatures (Also List on Line B of Recapitulation) ------------->		4208

Objections Not Ruled Upon for Lack of Jurisdiction:	
Forgery (F)	0
Similar Handwriting (SH)	0
Total Not Ruled Upon	0

BOARD OF ELECTIONS
IN THE CITY OF NEW YORK
32 Broadway
New York, NY 10004-1609
(212) 487-5300

PART II. RECAPITULATION

A. Number of Signatures Submitted for Candidate
B. Total Invalid Signatures
C. Total Valid Signatures (A minus B)
D. Number of Signatures Required **
** See footnotes on reverse.
See Reverse for County Committee

PART III. REFERRED TO BOARD

CLERK'S SIGNATURES:

Deputy Chief Clerk: [signature]

Deputy Chief Clerk: [signature]

PART IV. BOARD HEARING

Date:

Decision: ☐ In ☑ Out ☐ Reserve Decision

Memo:

Objector and/or Representative Present

Candidate and/or R

VOTE OF THE COMMISSIONERS

REPUBLICAN	YES	NO	N.V.
MN			
BX			
BK			
QN			
SI			

DEMOCRAT	YES	NO	N.V.
MN			
BX			
BK			
QN			
SI			

Exhibit F

Article in New York Daily News for July 22, 2013 stating that signatures for a rival Republican candidate John Burnett were accidentally shredded by workers for the Board of Elections but the candidate was allowed to reconstruct the signature pages and thereby get on the ballot

DAIL[illegible]S

CE[illegible]

DAILY P[illegible]TICS

"Miscommunicat[illegible]" L[illegible]YC Board Of Elections Shreddin[illegible] GOP Petitions

First the Brooklyn Board of Electio[illegible]old votes... and now they're shredding new signatures.

Mere weeks after the Daily News repor[illegible]post [illegible]ed votes [illegible]ns a Board worker in the same office mistak[illegible]2013 Republican [illegible]

It wasn't immediately clear Monday exa[illegible] signature sheets that are gathered to [illegible] ended up in the dustbin of electoral his[illegible]

"A single petition volume of 20 pages [illegible]ast Friday, Board spokeswoman Valerie Vazquez said in a statement res[illegible]uiry about the destroyed docs.

There's nothing short of an open civil w[illegible] of the Brooklyn GOP right now, so Republican politics in the borough a[illegible]he party faithful are mainly split between support of county Chairman C[illegible] Martin Golden.

Update: I am told by several GOP sou[illegible]tion carried the names of Joe Hynes for district attorney, John Burnet[illegible]s for the GOP county committee for the [illegible] (The me[illegible]e are important here because of their role in determining who serves as [illegible]ty.)

The current male district leader for the [illegible] was appointed the Brooklyn GOP Commissioner on the Board of El[illegible]power grab engineered by the Republican caucus of the City Council.

Update: I'm also to[illegible] workers from [illegible]volved in the Friday shredding incident. Both are Democrats. That in i[illegible]pically, petitions are watched over by a team -- one Democrat and o[illegible]

Regardless of party or borough, Board [illegible]y new to city voters.

W[illegible] that the 2012 electi[illegible]d yet again after a Board audit revealed 1,579 votes cast in Brooklyn [illegible]n pulled from the memory sticks that store data from the city's electronic [illegible]

Those votes were added to the grand t[illegible] batch of more than 400 votes cast in various parts of the city and dug [illegible] after last November's election.

Exhibit G

Typical example page from the approximately 500 pages of Specific Objections filed. This page is essentially blank except for the notations NR, NE and SWNE, SWNR

These notations mean Not Registered, Not Enrolled, Subscribing Witness Not Enrolled, Subscribing Witness Not Registered

These were false and spurious claims as all of the subscribing witnesses were registered to vote and nearly all the petition signers were registered to vote and in the Republican Party. The filing of these spurious claims shows that the objectors never bothered to look up the signatures to determine whether the voters and the witnesses were registered or not.

Objection Sheet

Line No. | **Reasons for Objections**

1
2
3
4
5
6
7
8 NR, NE
9
10
11
12
13
14
15
16
17
18
19
20

Objections to Statement of Witness:

SWNE, SWNR

Claimed Number of Signatures on Page: 10
Number of Invalid Signatures: 10
Number of Valid Signatures: 0

Petition ~~Sheet~~ Vol Number: NY13012
~~Bronx Volume~~ Sheet Number: 4

SUPREME COURT OF THE STATE OF NEW YORK
COUNTY OF NEW YORK: CIVIL TERM: PART 7

---X

SAMUEL H. SLOAN, RICHARD BOZULICH, THOMAS R. STEVENS,

Petitioners

Index No: 101087/2013

-against-

DANIEL S. SZALKIEWICZ, SALVATORE G. CARUSO, BOARD OF ELECTIONS IN THE CITY OF NEW YORK,

Respondents.

---X

60 Centre Street
New York, New York 10007
August 5, 2013

B E F O R E:

THE HONORABLE PAUL WOOTEN,
J U S T I C E

A P P E A R A N C E S:

SAMUEL H. SLOAN
Petitioner Pro Se
461 Peachtree Terrace
San Rafael, CA 94903

DANIEL S. SZALKIEWICZ, ESQ.
Attorney for Respondent Salvatore Caruso
280 Riverside Drive
New York, NY 10025

NEW YORK CITY LAW DEPARTMENT OFFICE OF THE CORPORATION COUNSEL
100 Church Street
New York, NY 10007
BY: Stephen Kitzinger, Esq.

BOARD OF ELECTIONS CITY OF NEW YORK
32 Broadway - 7th Floor
New York, NY 10004
BY: Steven H. Richman, Esq.

VANESSA MILLER
Senior Court Reporter

[illegible]

THE CO[illegible] case of Sloan versus Szalkiewicz, in [illegible] of 2013.

Who re[illegible]?

MR. SL[illegible] I'm representing myself.

THE CO[illegible]esents Mr. Szalkiewicz?

MR. SZ[illegible]Honor, I am Mr. Szalkiewicz and [illegible]dore G. Caruso who's actually the o[illegible]ure why I'm personally named.

THE CO[illegible]

MR. SZ[illegible] his counsel at the time and I guess my [illegible]ec as a contact individual.

THE CO[illegible]

MR. SZ[illegible] am Mr. Caruso's attorney as wel[illegible]

THE CO[illegible] well.

Any o[illegible]lkiewicz representing Mr. Caruso from [illegible]s?

MR. SL[illegible]jection to that, your Honor. But one [illegible] to is it's obvious that Mr. Caruso is a[illegible]ould like to know who's paying Mr. Szal[illegible]es because he's obviously got s[illegible] him who are doing this.

Proceedings

THE COURT: That's a request by you, sir?

MR. SLOAN: Yes, it is.

THE COURT: Your application is denied. We've never done that. In 30 years on the bench we've never, never -- I'm sorry. In five years on the bench and 27 years as an election law attorney, we've never had a case where that application's been granted. You have an exception, sir.

Who represents the Board?

MR. KITZINGER: Stephen Kitzinger, New York City Law Department.

MR. RICHMAN: Steven Richman, counsel for the respondent, Board of Elections.

THE COURT: Okay. Let the record reflect that I'm joined by Mr. Jack Suiter (ph), one of our principal law clerks who assists in this special election part.

All right. So was there a Board report here, sir?

MR. KITZINGER: Your Honor, there was a Board report but, initially, I believe there are three named plaintiffs and two of them are not present.

THE COURT: Okay.

MR. KITZINGER: So I think their claims should be dismissed.

THE COURT: Is Mr. Stevens here?

MR. SLOAN: No, he's not here.

THE COURT: Okay. Is Mr. Richard -- how do you --

MR. SLOAN: Bozulich. He's out of the country.

THE COURT: Okay. So two of the petitioners are not represented here today?

MR. SLOAN: That's correct, your Honor.

THE COURT: Okay. So do they plan to be represented? Do they have an attorney?

MR. SLOAN: I just don't know.

THE COURT: Okay. So you don't know if they're planning to be represented. I can't take your word that one of them is out of the country. I do know that the two are not here. It is now, approximately, 10:35. I will give them to 11:00 a.m. where I'll second-call the case to see if they appear.

But on your application, Mr. Sloan, which is an application for an order to validate to put you on the ballot for the Office Of Mayor of the City of New York on the Republican party for the September primary; is that correct?

MR. SLOAN: Yes, your Honor.

THE COURT: Very well. Have you served your affidavit of service?

MR. SLOAN: Yes, I have.

THE COURT: Do you have them?

MR. SLOAN: Yes, I do.

MR. KITZINGER: I have it too --

THE COURT: Just a moment. Let's go through procedure. Mr. Sloan.

(Handing.)

THE COURT: Okay. Officer Burgos, would you show the affidavit of service to the respondents please?

(Handing.)

MR. KITZINGER: I don't see an affidavit of service on the Board.

MR. SLOAN: Oh. They time-stamped it. It's in the back. I have to search for it. They have a time stamp from the Board of Elections.

THE COURT: One of them is time-stamped; isn't it?

MR. KITZINGER: Actually, I see time-stamped copies, I mean, if the Court is going to accept that.

THE COURT: Okay. At this particular time, I'm showing you the affidavit of service.

(Handing.)

THE COURT: Are there any objections to in personam jurisdiction?

MR. KITZINGER: None from the Board, your Honor.

Pr[illegible]

THE CO[illegible]

MR. S[illegible] [illegible]n, if I may, the only way I would object [illegible] n who actually served it on the Board, I [illegible] ndividual did it. If it was Mr. Sloan, [illegible] it in that he's actually a candidate and [illegible] he's unable to serve the Board personally. [illegible] ve an affidavit of service on behalf [illegible] 'd object until we can learn actually [illegible] individual that did it.

(Pause [illegible])

MR. S[illegible] Honor, if I may also, it's --

THE CO[illegible] ditional?

MR. S[illegible] it's my understanding and basis upon [illegible] lief that correspondence that was sent b[illegible], that he was additionally pr[illegible] himself that he left the court paper[illegible] at my office address. If he was the [illegible] either with him or left them himself, then I [illegible] testing the affidavit of service. And I [illegible] iolates the spirit of the law that th[illegible] s present and apparently questioned cert[illegible] the time of service.

THE CO[illegible] we have here is we have an affidavit of [illegible] orge Rankoth who said that I served this on August 21st at 7:45 --

MR. SLOAN: August 1st.

THE COURT: August 1st, 2013 at 7:45 a.m. --

MR. SLOAN: It should say p.m.

THE COURT: All right. It's not circled, but you're telling me it's meant to be 7:45 p.m.

And then there's a second affidavit of service that says 10:45 p.m., which is the petition. The mere fact that there's an allegation that one of the parties was present with the process server doesn't invalidate the service.

MR. SZALNIEWICZ: I'll waive the objection then.

THE COURT: Okay. That's number one.

So your objection to in personam jurisdiction on the basis of him being present then is inappropriate. The presumption is an affidavit of service creates a presumption which you have to rebut at the particular time. It's insufficient to rebut the presumption.

The question here is on the Board of Election case there is a Board of Election time stamp. In the past we have created that the Board of Election time stamp is the same as an affidavit which creates a presumption that it's properly served. If you wish to present evidence to rebut the Board of Election's service, you may do so. Okay. The mere fact that you claim you want to find out whether or not the candidate served the papers is, in my view, insufficient to rebut the presumption. If you have evidence that he served it or you wish to go to a Traverse, but to go on a fishing expedition is insufficient to rebut the presumption of the time stamp of the Board, which we normally accept because it is a City office.

MR. SZALKIEWICZ: Yes.

THE COURT: Okay. The in personam jurisdiction having been established, was there a Board report here?

MR. KITZINGER: Yes, your Honor. There was.

Since it's a citywide office, it would require 3,750 valid signatures. The Board found that the candidate has 89 valid signatures. There are 4,297 submitted, 4,208 of which were determined to be invalid. The vast majority were validated with the subscribing witness, was not enrolled in the Republican party, and this report was adopted unanimously by the Commissioner of Elections.

THE COURT: Could I see the Board report please?

MR. KITZINGER: Of course, your Honor.

THE COURT: Thank you.

(Handing.)

THE COURT: Mr. Sloan, do you have anything to say about the Board report?

MR. SLOAN: Yes. I have a great deal to say about this.

First place is this whole proceeding starts with a general objection signed by a Mr. Salvatore Caruso. Mr. Salvatore Caruso had three days to file this general objection, he then had another six days to file a specific objection. These specific objections contain completely different allegations than are on the Board report. The specific objections said that there were 4,269 signatures submitted, of which 4,200 were bad signatures, 69 were good signatures. These numbers are just pulled up out of the air. They just invented these numbers. It has no relationship to the truth. It was obvious that Mr. Caruso and Mr. Szalkiewicz never actually looked at the actual signature cards, never looked at the actual objections. They just made up this objection.

I have a copy of the specific objections right here. It's this big bundle of papers. I'd like to hand it up, if possible.

THE COURT: I'll take a look at that. Would you show it to your adversaries first to make sure that they agree that that is a proper copy of the specification [illegible]

MR. SI[illegible] document Mr. Szalkiewicz served on me, [illegible] at's the document.

THE CO[illegible] our theory to get back on the ballot?

MR. SI[illegible] s, number one, the specific object[illegible] fraudulent. They just made blanket st[illegible] the signatures except 69 -- I don't k[illegible] 69, are good and 4,200 were bad. This [illegible] Elections to the burden of spending a w[illegible] temporary workers and other people to [illegible] all of these signatures.

And th[illegible] very single page --

THE CO[illegible] there is a Board report.

MR. SI[illegible] ow that, your Honor, but --

THE CO[illegible] here is a Board report. The Board repor[illegible] ed 3,750 signatures to be found valid, [illegible] has 89. Tell me where you're going to [illegible] 's decision to get those signatures back [illegible]

MR. SI[illegible] my first point is the Board doesn't [illegible] hey submit a valid specific object[illegible] submit a specific objection, I'm on the ballot.

THE COURT: But did you have an opportunity to oppose that you thought that the specification objections were properly filed before the Board?

MR. SLOAN: Yes, I did. I said the same thing I'm saying here.

THE COURT: And did the Board rule?

MR. SLOAN: Well, what it comes down to in the end is the Board says that the only thing wrong with my petition is --

THE COURT: That's not what I asked you, Counsel -- that's not what I asked you, Mr. Sloan.

Did the Board of Elections rule that the specification of objections filed by the respondents were properly served?

MR. SLOAN: I don't think they actually ruled.

THE COURT: They had to, otherwise there wouldn't be a Board report.

MR. SLOAN: I'm not complaining about the service because, in fact --

THE COURT: Well, then they would've ruled that it's sufficient in its merit, otherwise there wouldn't be a Board report.

MR. SLOAN: But the Board report said something different than what the specific objection said.

THE COURT: So what?

MR. SLOAN: Because they should not have been allowed to -- if the specific objections contains false statements, such as none of the subscribing witnesses are registered to vote -- see, the specific objections says that none of the subscribing witnesses are objecting to it, all of the subscribing witnesses are; that's why I want you to look at those specific objections and you'll see --

THE COURT: I'm looking it, it says "SW" with "NE", Subscribing Witness Not Enrolled, subscribing witness is not registered.

MR. SLOAN: But, in fact, all of those witnesses are registered to vote. You have 500 sheets of paper saying that all of these subscribing witnesses are not registered to vote. In fact, every one of them are registered to vote. So you have 500, your Honor.

THE COURT: Did you pull the buff cards on each one of these SWs?

MR. SLOAN: Yes, I did.

THE COURT: Do you have certified copies to send to the Court?

MR. SLOAN: No, I don't.

THE COURT: So how are you going to prove your case?

MR. SLOAN: Well, the Board of Elections has the buff cards on all of these people.

THE COURT: Mr. Sloan, you have to go forward to prove your case. I'm asking for an offer of proof on how you intend to prove your case.

MR. SLOAN: Well, I can go to the Board of Elections and print out all of these buff cards of all these subscribing witnesses and show that they were all registered to vote.

THE COURT: Why haven't you already done that?

MR. SLOAN: It never occurred that this question would even come up because I assumed the Board of Elections would tell you that they're all registered to vote because the clerk's reports does not say that they were not registered to vote.

THE COURT: Okay. I will give you a shot.

Counsel, anything in opposition here?

MR. SZALKIEWICZ: Yeah. I'm sorry.

MR. KITZINGER: Your Honor, the vast majority is that they were not enrolled members of the Republican party; that is a requirement of the election law under 6-132(2).

THE COURT: I understand.

Is it your position that these people are not members of the Republican party?

[illegible]

MR. SI[illegible] [illegible] that they're not enrolled in the [illegible] but they were registered to [illegible]

THE CO[illegible] [illegible], then that defeats your case.

MR. SI[illegible] [illegible] I disagree, your Honor, because [illegible] didn't even know about this rule. It'[illegible]ly written rule. I don't think it'[illegible]chman starts --

THE CO[illegible] [illegible]'s stop.

In or[illegible]ominated to be the Republican part[illegible] Office Of Mayor, you have to be nomi[illegible] [illegible]eople.

MR. SI[illegible]

THE CO[illegible] [illegible]ers of the Republican party have to f[illegible]on; that's in the law; that's required[illegible]

MR. KI[illegible] [illegible]bdivision 2, your Honor.

MR. RI[illegible] [illegible], if we may, so it reads, "there s[illegible] [illegible] the bottom of each sheet a signed [illegible]itness who is a duly-qualified [illegible] and an enrolled voter of the same pol[illegible] [illegible] voter's qualified to sign the petiti[illegible]

THE CO[illegible] [illegible] Counsel?

MR. SLOAN: No, your Honor. My contention is -- first of all, I didn't know about that. But, secondly, that infringes the constitutional right to vote because it says "only." We're not talking about the people who signed the petition, we're just talking about the witnesses. It says the witnesses have to be Republicans. What is the reason why only Republicans are allowed to witness petitions? Why not Democrats, independents, socialists, greens, yellow people, black people, all kind of different people? It's an unreasonable rule.

There's no valid justification for the rule. All the rule does is stop the -- enable the Republican party, some interloper, like me for example, who I'm a registered Republican, I want to run for office and give the Republican hierarchy -- the insiders to the power to stop people like me, legitimate Republicans for a very long time, from running for office because they can control the subscribing witnesses because they have access to lots of people who do this kind of work for the Republican party and it's very hard for anybody else to come in and get witnesses. Remember, we're only talking about the witnesses --

THE COURT: Okay. Mr. Sloan, I think I get your point.

Is this the only offer of proof you have, sir?

MR. SLOAN: Well, again, I can get the buff cards --

THE COURT: No. I get your point.

So it's your position that your offer of proof to get you on the ballot is that while you concede that these subscribing witnesses are registered voters, and you also concede they are members of the Republican party --

MR. SLOAN: They're not members.

THE COURT: They're not members of the Republican party, but you believe there is a constitutional violation and I should rule on the constitutional violation to get you on the ballot.

MR. SLOAN: In other words, it infringes upon the constitutional right to petition the government. One, that's not constitutional --

THE COURT: I understand your point. Mr. Sloan, I understand your point. That argument's been made in at least three federal courts in the past ten years and it hasn't prevailed in any federal jurisdiction in the Second Circuit that I'm aware of.

However, I'll hear you in opposition.

MR. KITZINGER: Your Honor, as to the constitutional statement, the United States Court of

Appeals for the Second Circuit ruled in the case of Maslow versus the Board of Elections, at 658 F2d 291 -- I'm sorry, I think it's F3d, 291, 2011. That the specific provision, 6-132 subdivision 2 was valid and constitutionally affirmed. It relied in large measure in the United States Supreme Court case of Lopez V Torres which was handed down a couple of years prior. Also, the plaintiff, as in the Maslow case, sought certiori from the US Supreme Court and that was denied.

In addition, your Honor, there is a procedural problem to the extent that there is a facial challenge to the constitutionality of the provision. Upon information and belief, there's been no notice given to the Attorney General of the State of New York to defend or to provide him notice and an opportunity to defend the constitutionality of this provision.

THE COURT: Mr. Sloan, have you served the Attorney General of the State of New York?

MR. SLOAN: No, I have not, but I have served the Board of Elections which is an agency of the state.

THE COURT: Okay. Very well.

What we're going to do is we are going to wait until eleven o'clock. That will give us a chance to second call to see if Mr. Stevens and Mr. Bozulich appear.

So, ge [illegible] cond.

MR. K [illegible] nor, there's one last thing I'd like [illegible]

In Par [illegible] etition, there's a claim by the candidat [illegible] 'petitioners are new candidates who [illegible] d in the ballot before in any election [illegible] esignated circulating petitions for [illegible] on previously." In 2004, Mr. Sloan [illegible] be a candidate in what was then the 10 [illegible] istrict. That candidacy was unsuccessfu [illegible] ere were petitions submitted and t [illegible] n at minimum for the Eastern Distric [illegible] ing to validate that petition.

THE CO [illegible]

MR. S [illegible] your Honor, if I may, there's also, i [illegible] he ran on the libertarian lin [illegible] and submitted petitions as well.

Takin [illegible] should you reach the constitutional [illegible] hat is on Mr. Sloan's favor, what the [illegible] e on are the 1,473 objections to t [illegible] signatures that were on those that woul [illegible] he subscribing witnesses are not enrolle [illegible] these parties didn't even sign the petition to begin with and were not registered as a Republican party.

If we need to go this far, we'd like permission of the Court to either file a verified cross petition, which I have a copy of right here, or would have an answer likewise with an affirmative defense that the invalidating time period should be commenced in order to make sure that these remaining signatures are removed from the petition as well which would bring Mr. Sloan well below the [illegible],750 signatures he needs in order to be placed on the ballot.

THE COURT: The application that you're asking for, did you submit that as a counterclaim?

MR. SZALKIEWICZ: I did not submit it as a counterclaim, but I can, I have actually followed up in an answer, but I can change it in-between this call and the next call.

THE COURT: But the affirmative defense -- you have filed an affirmative defense to Mr. Sloan's petition?

MR. SZALKIEWICZ: I have it in front of me right now. I was planning on giving it up to the Court.

THE COURT: So you have not served it yet?

MR. SZALKIEWICZ: I have not. It's in front of me.

THE COURT: Because I didn't see it in my file.

MR. SLOAN: Your Honor, may I address the --

THE COURT: No. I hear it. That's all. This is all procedural.

We'll second-call this at, approximately, 11:10. So thank you.

(Case recalled.)

THE COURT: Okay. First of all, it is now 11:10 on August 5th. This matter having been called once for the 9:30 calendar now being second-called at the 11:00 a.m. calendar.

Mr. Stevens, Thomas Stevens, the petitioner, not having appeared and not having appeared pursuant to an attorney or proper representative. A Mr. Richard Bozulich, I'll spell it, B-O-Z-U-L-I-C-H, also a second petitioner not having appeared at the 9:30 call of the calendar, not having appeared at the second call of the calendar at 11:00 a.m., and having no legal or proper representative of same, the application on the order to show cause to validate is hereby dismissed for failure to appear.

In addition, the Court, having herein wishing to correct an error that it earlier made which would apply not only to Mr. Sloan who is here today, but to the other two petitioners, Mr. Bozulich and Mr. Stevens. According to the affidavit of service, there is an affidavit of service in which a Mr. George Rankoth, spelled R-A-N-K-O-T-H, properly served an order to show cause petition, an affidavit in support on the respondent, Daniel Szalkiewicz, and having also that same person having served an order to show cause affidavit in support on petition on Mr. Salvatore Caruso timely. However, the Board of Elections, according to the information put forward by Mr. Sloan that they were served with a copy of the validating petition, is timed-stamped properly. Also, they were served with a copy of the affidavit in support, but there is no time stamp that shows that Mr. Sloan properly served them with a copy of the order to show cause --

MR. SLOAN: I have the time stamp, your Honor.

THE COURT: Well, let me see it, sir.

(Pause in proceedings.)

MR. SLOAN: Your Honor, the Board of Elections keeps these records and they're not objecting and they don't claim that they weren't served. I don't see why I'm going through all these papers.

(Pause in proceedings.)

MR. SLOAN: I can't find it, but it's definitely at home. I definitely did serve. I definitely do have a time-stamped copy of it.

[illegible]

THE CO[illegible] time stamp of the order to show cause?

MR. SI[illegible] show cause, yes, but it's at home.

THE CO[illegible] serve them?

MR. SI[illegible] 4:35. In other words --

MR. KI[illegible] nor, we don't -- the Board doesn't [illegible] ceived it, but Mr. Sloan's stateme[illegible] is somewhat disturbing in light of Mr. [illegible] or argument, and --

THE CO[illegible] ake that as the generic "we." If you [illegible] ved it, if you believe that "he" meaning [illegible] as the candidates somehow served [illegible] cause, I'll take that he has jurisdictio[illegible] ave proof that he had served the orde[illegible] the order of the order to show cause.

MR. KI[illegible] hink he said "I", not "we."

THE CO[illegible] ot going to take that as testimony. He [illegible] ot going to hold it against him. [illegible] he did serve the order of the order to [illegible]

MR. KI[illegible] rd of Elections received a copy of each [illegible] ents.

THE COURT: Okay. Thank you, because I only have proof of two.

Very well. Thank you, Mr. Sloan.

Okay. I've heard the application under the offer of proof, and I have the Board report. And under the Board report which says that the number of signatures submitted by Mr. Sloan was 4,297, the total number of invalid signatures was 4,208 - I'm sorry, yeah, 4,208, the total valid was 89 and the number of signatures required was 3,[illegible]. Under that application, I've asked for an offer of proof and Mr. Sloan has come forward that he wishes to rely solely on the argument that certain SWs should be reversed by this Court because of the requirement that those SWs be enrolled members of the party.

Under this situation, Mr. Sloan also admits that he was aware of the requirement that members of the party, Republican party had to be SWs. In addition to that, he now raises as his sole application a constitutional claim that the requirement under the election law that requires that the SWs on the designating petition be enrolled members of the representative party, however, that application for a constitutional claim is jurisdictionally defective because under the rules of the court, if you make a constitutional claim in state court, you must serve the Attorney General. And in this particular case, you would've had to serve the Attorney General before the last day to bring the order to show cause to designate a ballot, which was on July 25, 2013.

Having admitted that you haven't served the Attorney General renders the constitutional claim jurisdictionally defective and, therefore, it is denied based on the offer of proof that this is the only claim that you have to reverse the position of the Board that is prima facie defective. It is insufficient proof here to even proceed on an order to show cause -- on the line-by-line order to show cause based on your representations here in court. Therefore, the order to show cause, an application to validate, is hereby denied.

You can order the transcript in which I will so-order the transcript in this period if you wish to proceed and appeal this matter to the First Department. Understand that the First Department will be hearing all appeals on August 12 and August 13, which is next week, so, therefore, ordering the transcript should be expeditious to you.

MR. SLOAN: Yes. I do wish to order the transcript and I will appeal.

THE COURT: Okay. Very well, sir.

Anything else, Counsel?

MR. SLOAN: Yes, your Honor, I would like to address one more issue that we didn't do yet, and that is I'm certain that the signature of Mr. Caruso on the specific objection is a forgery because the signatures are so totally different from the voter registration card. He signed it one way --

THE COURT: Excuse me, sir. I'm not even hearing this application now. I asked for your offer of proof earlier, you didn't even mention this. Now that I've ruled, you want to come up with something new.

MR. SLOAN: No --

THE COURT: No, no. I'm not going to permit you to put that on the record when I asked you what was your offer of proof, sir.

So please, Mr. Sloan, I've ruled. You're obviously an intelligent gentleman. You're reserving your rights for an appeal.

Anything else?

MR. SZALKIEWICZ: Just that a verified answer has been served on the Board and Mr. Sloan -- two others were put in the mail, two other named respondents.

THE COURT: We do have the answer which you handed up today. I point out the answer does not have any counterclaims in it, which would have to be served before July 25t[illegible] ral denial.

I do [illegible] reserve the right to somehow bring [illegible] tions, whether that's appropriate or [illegible] nother time, I don't believe so, but [illegible] en ruled on. This matter is adjou[illegible].

MR. K[illegible] ou, your Honor.

MR. R[illegible] your Honor.

[illegible]**********

CERTIFIED TO BE A [illegible] RANSCRIPT OF THE ORIGINAL STENOGRAPH[illegible] F THIS PROCEEDING.

____
[illegible] ER
[illegible] Reporter

SUPREME COURT OF THE STATE OF NEW YORK
COUNTY OF NEW YORK

Sam Sloan,
Richard Bozulich,
Thomas R. Stevens

Index No. 101087/13

Petitioners,

-against-

Daniel S. Szalkiewicz,
Salvatore G. Car[illegible]
Board of Elections in the City of New York,

Respondents.

AFFIDAVIT IN SUPPORT OF PETITION FOR REHEARING

STATE OF NEW YORK

SS

COUNTY OF NEW YORK

Samuel H. Sloan, being duly sworn, deposes and says:

1. I make this affidavit in support of a petition for rehearing. No prior application has been made for the relief requested herein except for those applications made at the hearing on August 5, 2013. Because I did not previously know what defenses would be made in opposition to my order to show cause, I did not know and could not have known that the Board of Elections would defend its actions based in its interpretation of Section 6-132 (2) of New York Election Law. Also, it did not appear that the court fully understood the facts and circumstances of this case. I want to preserve these issues for appeal, if necessary.

2. Here in summary are my objections to the decision of the Board of Elections in the City of New York dated July 31, 2013 to kick me and the two other candidates off the ballot.

3. The Specific Objections that resulted in me and two other candidates being thrown off the ballot were improperly filed and thus should not have been considered. Sal Caruso who is purported to be the specific objector is an elderly man approaching 70 who lives in the most remote area of New York City, the Throngs Neck section of the Bronx near the land's end. He was apparently selected to be the front man because of the remoteness of his situation and the difficulty in serving him. When asked why he got involved in this case, Sal Caruso replied, "I am a member of the Republican Party and they asked me to help out." This tells us what we knew already which is that he is not the real objector and is just doing this as a favor to somebody else or possibly as a result of being paid to do this. This should not be allowed and the real objectors should be revealed and disclosed.

4. In comparing the signature on the General Objections with the signature on the Specific Objections it is obvious that the two documents do not match and were not signed by the same person and thus one of them is a forgery. The Voter Registration Card for Salvatore Caruso is on file with the Bronx Board of Elections. In comparing the signatures, the signature on the Voter Registration

Card is similar to the signature on the General Objection and both are completely different from the signature on the Specific Objection.

5. Sal Caruso was personally served with the Order to Show Cause and the petition and affidavit in support at his residence at 540 Ellsworth Avenue, Apartment C-1, Bronx New York, at 10:45 PM on the same day that the Order to Show Cause was signed. He was specifically told that his appearance was required on Monday at 9:30 AM in Room 341 at 60 Centre Street on August 5, 2013. Nevertheless he defaulted and did not appear. In view of questions raised as to whether he actually signed the "Specific Objections" with the Board of Elections in the City of New York, he should be held in default and required to appear and/or my candidates should be restored to the ballot.

6. The Sal Caruso who filed these General Objections and Specific Objections was and is said to be represented by attorney Daniel S. Szalkiewicz, PC, 280 Riverside Drive, New York, NY 10025. Mr. Daniel S. Szalkiewicz is a hard man to find. Although he advertises his office as at 280 Riverside Drive, New York NY 10025, I visited that address and the doorman informed me that there are no offices there. It is a simple apartment building. Also, the name of Daniel S. Szalkiewicz is not on either the building directory or any of the mail boxes. His actual apartment number or office number is not provided in any directory of lawyers. Lawyers in New York are required to maintain an office and to be there most of the time.

Daniel S. Szalkiewicz by not [illegible] e or apartment where he can be located is in violati[illegible] It is also highly probable that Mr. Daniel S. [illegible] the forger of the signature of Mr. Sal Caruso [illegible] ections, as it appears that the same pen was used t[illegible] nd address of Daniel S. Szalkiewicz as was used to s[illegible] nature of Sal Caruso.

7. Rather than provide line-[illegible] bjections, the objectors claimed that there [illegible] es but only 69 were good and the other 4200 were [illegible] ors simply marked virtually all of the approxi[illegible] petition sheets with SWNR and marked virtually al[illegible] NR, NE. SWNR means Subscribing Witness not Regi[illegible] false and spurious claims as all of the subscri[illegible] e registered to vote. The filing of these spurious [illegible] the objectors never bothered to look up the sign[illegible] e whether the voters and the witnesses were regis[illegible]

8. It was quickly establishe[illegible] s were not true. All of the Subscribing witnesses ar[illegible] red to vote in the State of New York. Once this [illegible] t should have been evident that the Specific Ob[illegible] ous and frivolous and the objectors had never both[illegible] e actual signature cards on file with the Board [illegible] objectors simply sought to require the Board [illegible] he candidates to do all

the work to prove the validity of the petitions. This shifting of the Burden of Proof was improper and should not have been allowed.

9. Nevertheless, the Board of Elections went ahead with validating the petitions, expending considerable time and effort and resources to do so. The end result was that only 112 of the signers were found to be not registered to vote and only 59 of the more than 4000 signers were found to be not registered as Republicans. These numbers were completely different from the numbers claimed by the objectors.

10. However, the Board of Elections found that in the cases of 3905 of the signatures, although the signers were registered Republicans, the subscribing witnesses were not registered Republicans. In short, the signatures were good, but the subscribing witnesses were not good because they were not Republicans.

11. It is an interpretation of New York Election although not specifically stated in the law that the witness to the petition must also be in the same political party in New York as the signers. The petitioners herein were not aware of this interpretation at the time of circulating the petitions. Petitioners also believe that this is not strictly speaking what the law says and in any case is Constitutionally invalid in that it deprives the petition signers and the candidates of the Constitutional Right to Petition the Government and has no rational basis. It deprives the signers of the petitioner

of the right to nominate candidates of their own choosing.

12. Section 132 (2) of New York Election law provides the following:

> 2. There shall be appended at the bottom of each sheet a signed statement of a witness who is a duly qualified voter of the state and an enrolled voter of the same political party as the voters qualified to sign the petition, and who is also a resident of the political subdivision in which the office or position is to be voted for. However, in the case of a petition for election to the party position of member of the county committee, residence in the same county shall be sufficient. Such a statement shall be accepted for all purposes as the equivalent of an affidavit, and if it contains a material false statement, shall subject the person signing it to the same penalties as if he or she had been duly sworn. The form of such statement shall be substantially as follows:
>
> STATEMENT OF WITNESS
>
> I,.................... (name of witness) state: I am a duly qualified voter of the State of New York and am an enrolled voter of the...................... party. I now reside at...................
> (residence address).

13. This law is obviously unconstitutional as applied in the circumstances of this case because it deprives the petition signers of the First Amendment right to petition the Government. The First Amendment states:

> Congress shall make no law respecting an establishment of religion, or prohibiting the free exercise thereof; or abridging the freedom of speech, or of the press; or the right of the people peaceably to assemble, and to petition the government for a redress of grievances.

14. It is difficult to imagine a more blatant and obvious violation of a Constitutional Right than to make a rule that one may not petition the Government unless the petition is witnessed by

Republicans!! What nonsense!!!!

15. It was not until the hearing on Monday August 5 that it became apparent that the court dismissed all the other objections to the ruling of the Board of Elections and that this case might rest entirely on the Constitutionality of Section 6-132 (2) of New York Election Law. As the court correctly pointed out, I had not yet served the New York Attorney General with notice that the Constitutionality of a New York Law was at issue. However, immediately after the hearing on August 5, 2013, I served a complete set of papers on the office of the Attorney General at 120 Broadway. Since then I have written and served a detailed letter to the Attorney General explaining why Section 6-132 (2) of New York Election Law is Unconstitutional as applied in this case. A copy of my letter is annexed hereto and marked Exhibit A. Note that it shows a time stamp by the Attorney General's office and by the office of the Board of Elections in the City of New York.

16. There can be little doubt that Specific Objections filed by attorney Daniel S. Szalkiewicz, PC, 280 Riverside Drive, New York, NY 10025 includes a forgery. The signatures simply do not match. Not only is it a forgery, but it is a very poor forgery. He cannot even get that done right. Since the court has declined to address this issue, I have written letters to the Manhattan DA and the Bronx DA complaining about this. Copies of these letters are annexed hereto as

Exhibits B and C.

17. At the hearing on August [illegible] for the Board of Elections stated that the Co[illegible] Election Law Section 6-132 (2) has been upheld in [illegible]es. I have since located two of those cases a[illegible]tions to them are irrelevant to this case. Bas[illegible] concern a bunch of Democrats who want to invade [illegible] Republican Party by circulating petitions to get [illegible] disruptive candidates into the Republican Primarie[illegible] cases did these Democrats actually circulate [illegible] They just brought actions for declaratory reli[illegible]ed for good reasons.

18. Although counsel for the [illegible] claimed that the Constitutionality of this la[illegible]n three federal cases, this is not true. It was dec[illegible]onal in Lerman v. Bd. of Elections of N.Y.C., 232 [illegible] Cir. 2000). Nevertheless, that statute h[illegible] and the Board of Elections in the City of New [illegible] enforce it, as I found out on August 5.

19. In the case presented he[illegible]red Republican. I recruited a slate of candida[illegible]egistered Republicans to run for Citywide offices. [illegible] petition signatures were collected and timely fi[illegible] of Elections in the

City of New York at [illegible] Broadway.

20. We thought everything was hunky-dory and were taken by surprise when I received a call on Sunday July 28 from Anthony Ribustello, a clerk in the Bronx Board of Elections, informing me that almost all of my signatures were considered invalid solely because they had not been "witnessed" by an enrolled member of the Republican Party. Previously, I thought that any credible person could witness a petition signature. I did not know that there were restrictions and limitations on who could collect or submit the petition signatures.

21. My Candidates were kicked off the ballot on July 31, 2013. I filed suit in New York Supreme Court, New York County, the following day.

22. At a hearing on August 5 before Judge Paul Wooten of Manhattan State Supreme Court, I learned that the Board of Elections in the City of New York was using New York Election Law 6-132 (2) as the sole basis for declaring 3905 of my signatures to be invalid, since the witnesses to those petitions were not registered Republicans. I did not personally know any of the petition gatherers except that I met them during the last few hours on the last day of the petition drive, when they turned in their signatures. However, I have since looked them up on the records of the Board of Elections and I have found them to be a mixture of Democrats, Libertarians and Blanks. All

of them are registered voters. Mostly they seem to be people who have little interest in politics but who gather petition signatures as a means of employment. Some of them needed hotel rooms as they seemed to be homeless. Several of them defected to Spitzer during the last hours of the petition drive, after it was reported on TV that Spitzer was paying $800 per day to those who would collect signatures for him. This is a matter that should be investigated.

23. The main case cited by Counsel for the Board of Elections is Maslow v. Board of Elections in City of N.Y., 658 F.3d 291 (2d Cir. 2011) citing N.Y. State Bd. of Elections v. Lopez-Torres, 552 U.S. 196, 128 S.Ct. 791, 798, 169 L.Ed.2d 665 (2008)

24. However, the Maslow case is completely different from the case presented here. The Maslow case involved Democrats who wanted to register Republicans to run as Republican candidates. For example a bunch of Democrats could collect and submit petitions on behalf of a candidate who is likely to be disruptive to the opponent's elections. Naturally, the Republicans would want these people kept out.

25. However, in my case the petitioners were a random collection of semi-homeless Democrats, Libertarians and Blanks who were unemployed and simply wanted a job. They had no idea about raiding an opposing party. In the Maslow case, Lori Maslow, the good wife, wanted to be able to circulate petitions on behalf of her husband, Aaron Maslow,

should he ever decide to run for election as a Republican, even though she is a Democrat. She claimed the Constitutional Right to Associate with the Republican Party even though she was not a member of that Party. Her application was frivolous and failed for obvious reasons.

26. In fact, Aaron Maslow has never run for office as a Republican and Lori Maslow has never circulated petitions for him as a Democrat, so there was no actual case or controversy. Aaron Maslow is one of the most active litigators of election law cases. He has also served as Chairman of the Nomination Committees for both the Republicans and the Democrats at the same time. I like to say that the neighborhood where I live has Democracy as we have both the Crips and the Bloods. Maslow's case is better or worse as he works for both the Republicans and the Democrats, switching back and forth.

27. In the case presented here, however, 3905 Republicans signed petitions believing that they were nominating candidates to run for office as Republicans. The 3905 people who signed the petitions did not know the witnesses or even who the witnesses would be. They all just naturally assumed that their petitions were valid.

28. It is the constitutional rights of the petitioners that have been infringed. In the Maslow case there were no petitioners because no such petitions had actually been circulated. The Maslow case was

merely an action for declara[illegible]d not occur in the context of an actual controv[illegible]ase lasted 5 years. It started in 2006 and continue[illegible]

29. The First Amendment to t[illegible]ovides: Congress shall make no law respecting an es[illegible]igion, or prohibiting the free exercise thereof; o[illegible]eedom of speech, or of the press; or the right of t[illegible] to assemble, and to petition the government for [illegible]ances. Here the law clearly infringes the Consti[illegible] petition the government". No plaintiff in [illegible]serted that right because no petition was actu[illegible]d thus there were no petitioners.

30. The provision relied upo[illegible]Elections has already been declared unconstitution[illegible]man v. Bd. of Elections of N.Y.C., 232 F.3d 135, 145 [illegible]hat decision struck down the sentence cited by t[illegible]ons, yet they shamelessly quoted and read [illegible]statute during the hearing on August 5. Althoug[illegible]fers to the residency requirement, the residency r[illegible]he same sentence as the requirement that a witness m[illegible] the same political party and the same logic and [illegible] Nevertheless, the statute has not been amended [illegible]ey read the sentence in full in the hearing before J[illegible]

31. The Maslow case was pending before the courts for five years, because there was no live controversy and there was no rush to decide it. In the case here, however, the Primary Election will be held on September 10. Either the candidates will be on it, or they will not be on it, so a final decision must be made by that time.

32. It was not until the hearing yesterday that it became apparent that the constitutionality of the Election Law would be the main issue of the case. I raised or attempted to raise other issues, including the apparent forgery of the signature of Salvatore Caruso on the Specific Objections. I also objected to the appearance of Daniel Szalkiewicz as counsel for Salvatore Caruso when it is obvious that Sal Caruso, who is an elderly man approaching 70, is not the real objector and is merely a front man for the undisclosed real objector.

33. It is obvious that New York Election Law 6-132 (2) is unconstitutional as applied in this case. Here, we have 3905 voters who signed a petition thinking that it would be submitted to the Board of Elections and the names of the candidates nominated would be on the ballot. The signers did not know anything about the subscribing witnesses and had no connection with them. They did not even know their names much less their political affiliations. It is clear that the 3905 signers of the petitions have the First Amendment

constitutional right to petition and these rights have been infringed on the pretext that the witnesses with whom they have no connection are not Republicans. Frankly, this situation is so unconstitutional that I believe that you will not be able to defend it.

34. It is apparently the interpretation of the Board of Elections in the City of New York that the above provision implies that the party of the subscribing witness must be the same as the party of the signer of the petition. However, the above provision does not actually say that. It says that the signer must be an "Enrolled" member. An "Enrolled Member" could be a member of the Republican Party in Pennsylvania and in fact Maslow is planning to file a case saying exactly that. An Enrolled member could be a member of the Republican National Committee. It could even be somebody who has read and studied Plato's Republic and has joined an email group to study and discuss the Republican ideals as set forth in that famous book. In short, the average person reading this law would not reach the same conclusion that the Board of Elections reaches.

WHEREFORE, for all of the reasons set forth above, Petitioner prays that this petition for a rehearing be granted and upon hearing

(a) That an order be entered reinstating Sam Sloan, Richard Bozulich and Thomas R. Stevens as candidates on the ballot in the coming elections

(b) That this matter be referred to the District Attorney's office to investigate the apparent and obvious forgery of the signature of Salvatore G. Caruso on the Specific Objections.

____
Samuel H. Sloan

Sworn to Before me this 7th
Day of August 2013

____
NOTARY PUBLIC

____
Samuel H. Sloan
1664 Davidson Avenue, Apt. 1B
Bronx NY 10453

917-507-7226
917-659-3397
samhsloan@gmail.com

STATE OF NEW YORK)
) ss
COUNTY OF NEW YORK)

VE[illegible]

I, the undersigned, the peti[illegible] foregoing petition, being duly sworn, says:

I have read the foregoing pe[illegible] by me and know the contents thereof and the sam[illegible] knowledge, except as to those matters herein stat[illegible]pon information and belief and as to those matte[illegible] be true.

____

[illegible]ure of Petitioner

On the 7th Day of August, 20[illegible]nally came Samuel H. Sloan to me known to be the [illegible]erein and who executed the foregoing instrument. Su[illegible]re to such instrument before me and duly acknowled[illegible]ed the same.

____

NOTARY PUBLIC

Exhibit A

General Notice to the Attorney General's Office that the Constitutionality of a New York Law is at issue in this case

Exhibit B

Complaint to the Manhattan District Attorney regarding an apparent forgery in the Specific Objections

Exhibit C

Complaint to the Bronx District Attorney regarding an apparent forgery in the Specific Objections

Exhibit D

Time Stamped Copy showing service [illegible] in the City of New York at 4:32 P.M. on August [illegible]

(included because it was [illegible] the last hearing)

New York County Clerk's
Index No. 10108[illegible]

To be argued by
Stephen Kitzinger
(15 Minutes)

NEW YORK SUPREME COURT
APPELLATE DIVISION: FIRST DEPARTMENT

SAM SLOAN, RICHARD BOZULICH, THOMAS R. STEVENS,

Petitioners-Appellants,

-against-

DANIEL [illegible] SZALKIEWICZ, SALVATORE G. CARUSO, BOARD OF ELECTIONS IN THE CITY OF NEW YORK;

Respondents-Respondents.

BRIEF OF RESPONDENTS' BOARD OF ELECTIONS

MICHAEL A. CARDOZO,
Corporation Counsel of the
City of New York,
Attorney for Respondent
Board of Elections,
100 Church Street, 2-126
New York, New York 10007.
(212) 356-2087
skitzing@law.nyc.gov

Stephen Kitzinger
Of Counsel

August 12, 201[illegible]

TABLE OF CONTENTS

TABLE OF AUTHORITIES

Cases **Pages**

Statutes

NEW [illegible]
APPELLATE D[illegible] [illegible]ARTMENT

[illegible] SLOAN, R[illegible] [illegible]HOMAS R.
[illegible]

[illegible]-Appellants,

[illegible]

DANIEL S. SZALE[illegible] [illegible]G. CARUSO,
BOARD OF ELECT[illegible] [illegible] NEW YORK;

[illegible]espondents.

[illegible]BRIEF FOR RE[illegible] [illegible]LECTIONS

PRE[illegible]

Petitioners-Appe[illegible] [illegible] a decision and order of the Supreme Court, Ne[illegible] [illegible]oten, J.S.C.), dated August 9, 2012, that den[illegible] [illegible]pellants' petition to validate their designati[illegible] [illegible]ng placement on the ballot for the public of[illegible] [illegible]mptroller, and Public Advocate, respectively in [illegible] 2012 Republican Party Primary Electio[illegible] (the "Pri[illegible]

QUESTIONS PRESENTED

Did Supreme Court properly deny petitioners-appellants' application to validate petition signatures that were witnessed and subscribed by individuals who are not enrolled members of the Republican Party?

STATEMENT OF FACTS

On or about July 11, 2013, petitioners-appellants filed a combined designating petition (the "Designating Petition") and a cover sheet with the Board of Elections purporting to designate them as candidates for the Republican Party nomination for the public offices of Mayor, Comptroller, and Public Advocate, respectively. Salvatore Caruso ("Caruso") timely filed and served an objection to the Designating Petition alleging, inter alia, that the vast majority of the signatures contained in the Designating Petition were witnessed and subscribed to by individuals who are not enrolled members of the Republican Party.

The Board's staff conducted its review of the objection and produced a Clerks' Report that recommended that the Board determine that of the approximately 4,297 signatures on the petition, only 89 were valid. Of the 4,208 invalid signatures, 3,905 were recommended to be determined invalid because the subscribing witness was not an enrolled member of the Republican Party. Thereafter, at a duly noticed hearing of the Commissioners of Elections in the City of New York, the Board adopted the Clerks' Report and determined that the Designating Petition was invalid as it contained an insufficient number of valid signatures to qualify for the placement of any of the petitioners-appellants' names on the ballot in the Primary Election.

Petitioners-appellants timely commenced the proceeding below. On the return date, only petitioner-appellant Sloan (who is not an attorney) appeared for petitioners-appellants. Supreme Court (Wooten, J.S.C.) dismissed the claims of petitioner-appellants Bozulich and Stevens for failing to appear. *See* Transcript, p. 20. Supreme Court further dismissed petitioner-appellant Sloan's petition on the basis that he brought a facial challenge to N.Y. Election Law § 6-132(2) but failed to notify the Attorney General of this claim. *See* Transcript, p. 24.

DECI[illegible]

Decision New Y[illegible] [illegible]n, J.S.C.) dismissed petitioner-appellant's v[illegible] [illegible]ing, stating, inter alia, that

> "Having ad[illegible] t[illegible] haven't served the [illegible] renders the [illegible] claim jurisdictio[illegible] and, therefore, [illegible] based on the offer [illegible] is the only claim [illegible] reverse the positi[illegible] that is prima fac[illegible] It is insufficie[illegible] even proceed on [illegible] cause – on the li[illegible] to show cause base[illegible] cations here in [illegible], the order to s[illegible] cation to validat[illegible]..

The instant appe[illegible]

Applicable Rule

N.Y. Election Law § 6-132 states, inter alia:

§ 6-132. Designating petition; form

2. There shall be appended at the bottom of each sheet a signed statement of a witness who is a duly qualified voter of the state and an enrolled voter of the same political party as the voters qualified to sign the petition, and who is also a resident of the political subdivision in which the office or position is to be voted for. However, in the case of a petition for election to the party position of member of the county committee, residence in the same county shall be sufficient.

N.Y. Civil Practice Law & Rule 1012 state, inter alia:

Rule 1012. Intervention as of right; notice to attorney-general, city, county, town or village where constitutionality in issue.

(b) Notice to attorney-general, city, county, town or village where constitutionality in issue.

> 1. When the constitutionality of a statute of the state, or a rule and regulation adopted pursuant thereto is involved in an action to which the state is not a party, the attorney-general, shall be notified and permitted to intervene in support of its constitutionality.

ARGUMENT

N.Y. ELECTION LAW § 6-132(2) IS CONSTITUTIONAL.

Section 6-132(2) of the Election Law is constitutional. The United States Court of Appeals for the Second Circuit explicitly upheld the "party witness" rule found in § 6-132(2) in *Maslow v. Board of Elections*, 658 F.3d 291, 298-99 (2d Cir. 2011) ("As Plaintiffs have not demonstrated any non-trivial burden to their First Amendment rights, we need not closely analyze New York's justification for the Party Witness Rule. We only note that the State has a legitimate interest in protecting its political parties from party raiding, *see Rosario*, 410 U.S. at 760-62, which was clearly contemplated by members of the State Legislature when the Rule was adopted. The Party Witness Rule helps combat party raiding by denying hostile non-party elements access to one part of a political party's nomination process.").

Petitioners challenge the constitutionality of ° 6-132(2) alleging that it is violative of their right to petition the government protected by the First Amendment to the United States Constitution. Petitioners-appellants have offered no reason to disregard the Second Circuit's ruling in Maslow finding this provision constitutional. Moreover, petitioner-appellant is simply incorrect in his recitation of the facts and circumstances surrounding the retention of the party witness rule post *Lerman v. Board of Elections*, 232 F.3d 135 (2d Cir. 2000). Following *Lerman*, the legislature amended § 6-132 to remove the requirement that a subscribing witness be eligible to vote for the candidate appearing on the petition. The legislature elected to retain the party witness rule.

Lastly, petitioner-appellants confuse and conflate the terms registration and enrollment. Registration refers to the administrative process by which one makes oneself eligible to vote, *see* N.Y. Election Law § 5-100, whereas enrollment refers to the election to join a recognized political party. *See* N.Y. Election Law § 5-300, *et seq*.

As the subscribing witnesses were, admittedly, not enrolled members of the Republican Party, they were ineligible to serve as subscribing witnesses on the Designating Petition. Accordingly, the order of the Supreme Court should be affirmed.

CON[illegible]

FOR ALL [illegible], **THE ORDER OF** [illegible] **SHOULD BE AFFIRMED** [illegible]

[illegible]ted,

[illegible]
[illegible] of the
[illegible]
[illegible]dent
[illegible]s

[illegible] ______________________________
[illegible]itzinger

STEPHEN KITZINGER,
Of Counsel.

PRINTING SPECIFICATIONS STATEMENT

I hereby certify pursuant to 22 N.Y.C.R.R. § 600.10.3(f) that this brief was prepared on a computer, using Courier New 12, with double-spacing for the body and single-spacing for footnotes. The entire brief contains 1,390 words, not including portions that may be excluded from the count pursuant to 22 N.Y.C.R.R. § 600.10.3(a)(3).

Dated: New York, New York
August , 2013

MICHAEL A. CARDOZO
Corporation Counsel of the
City of New York
Attorney for Respondent-Respondent
By: Stephen Kitzinger
Assistant Corporation Counsel
100 Church Street, 2-126
New York, New York 10007

By: ______________________
Stephen Kitzinger

Made in the USA
Monee, IL
05 November 2026

67375834R00066